Ph.D. Completion and Attrition:

Policies and Practices
to Promote Student Success

Ph.D. Completion and Attrition:
Policies and Practices to Promote Student Success

Ph.D. Completion Project Staff:

Robert S. Sowell, Vice President, Programs and Operations

Nathan E. Bell, Director, Research and Policy Analysis

Sheila Nataraj Kirby, Consultant, CGS

ISBN: 1-933042-26-5

Printed in the United States

TABLE OF CONTENTS

FOREWORD

By Debra W. Stewart, President, Council of Graduate Schools

This volume is the fourth in the series of monographs developed by the Council of Graduate Schools (CGS) over the course of the Ph.D. Completion Project. The first two, *Ph.D. Completion and Attrition: Analysis of Baseline Program Data from the Ph.D. Completion Project* (CGS, 2008a), and *Ph.D. Completion and Attrition: Analysis of Baseline Demographic Data from the Ph.D. Completion Project* (CGS, 2008b) presented baseline data on the institutions partnering with CGS in the Ph.D. Completion Project and their Ph.D. completion rates over time, by broad discipline field and by student demographics. The third volume, *Ph.D. Completion and Attrition: Findings from Exit Surveys of Ph.D. Completers*, added a crucial component to the study—the graduate student's perspective—by examining data from the exit surveys administered to graduates of participating doctoral programs at these universities. The current volume, *Ph.D. Completion and Attrition: Policies and Practices to Promote Student Success*, gives specific attention to the institutional policies developed at partner institutions, which have great potential to affect completion at the institutions involved in this project.

Because these volumes reflect a carefully sequenced project, we recommend that the four publications in the Ph.D. Completion Project be read in order. However, realizing that in some instances only the most recent publication may be available, or of interest, to certain readers, I provide here some general context for the project as a whole and describe the place of this volume within it.

It was the stature and the costliness of the doctoral enterprise that motivated the graduate community in the mid-1990s to launch a self-examination directed at identifying areas of weakness and at generating strategies for addressing them. The result has been a proliferation of studies and reports on doctoral education in the United States. These reports focused on various disciplines, subsets of graduate students, time frames for completion, and on the efficacy of different interventions (CGS, 2004). By 2003, it was clear that all of this work provided a rich stew for creative speculation about how doctoral education might be further strengthened, a context that was essential for motivating the extremely successful U.S. system to realize that it could benefit from enhancements. It was also clear that the time had come for CGS to launch a national initiative that would result in firming up a foundation for specific best-practice recommendations to U.S. graduate schools, programs, funders, and policymakers.

But to move forward two things needed to happen. First, the community needed to agree on a common empirical measurement for assessing positive change. And second, in selecting that mode of measurement, we needed to settle on a "number," a concrete variable that would help unpack a variety of issues emerging from the past decade of discussion and scholarship. We settled on student completion and attrition rates from Ph.D. programs as the key point of leverage to generate best-practice recommendations that would ultimately improve the effectiveness of American Ph.D. programs.

Completion was an ideal measurement because it could be calculated in a straightforward, transparent and noncontroversial fashion for all doctoral programs. But more importantly, a decade of critical reflection within the higher education community had already highlighted the need to improve completion rates as one of the most urgent issues affecting doctoral education. We hoped that if we could launch a project that would empower all stakeholders, especially the deans of U.S. graduate schools, to lead conversations with faculty and students about what the completion and attrition rates actually were, and about what kinds of interventions might most successfully be implemented to improve completion, those efforts alone would move the conversation forward. But if, in addition, we could also study a carefully selected set of interventions, specifically designed to address attrition in clearly defined disciplinary, programmatic, and university settings, we could generate the information upon which solid best-practice recommendations could be provided by CGS to our membership community. The Ph.D. Completion Project is aiming to achieve that objective.

Most readers familiar with CGS publications will notice that this monograph, unlike the three previous publications in its series, begins to take a wider view of the institutional factors and interventions that have been used to improve completion rates and reduce attrition. While a comprehensive report on "best practices" for improving Ph.D. completion will not be available until the culminating book in this project is published, the current volume lays the groundwork for this final publication by providing detailed descriptions of interventions as well as "promising practices" provided in initial reports from participating universities.

Once again, we must stress the caveat that we offered in the first three volumes of this series. The information detailed here was provided by institutions selected in a national competition that invited graduate schools to record their own histories of completion. Universities were asked to record completion and attrition by demographic group within broad fields, to craft strategies to address concerns, and to implement those strategies, measuring their impacts, in part through continued tracking of student completion across demographic groups. Participants were selected for inclusion based on their demonstrated commitments to carrying through with these tasks. For this reason, our sample may show a bias toward universities and graduate schools committed to the mission of understanding and acting upon the challenge of increasing completion rates and systematically addressing differentials across demographic groups. While we do not claim that this data set represents the full range of completion-related practices and policies used by doctorate-granting universities or programs in the United States, it does represent a set of institutions that are broadly representative of doctoral-granting institutions: public and private, large and small, and geographically dispersed, with reasonably diverse missions regarding doctoral education.

In conclusion, this volume will be an illuminating first look into a set of innovative strategies designed to improve completion rates at a wide range of institutions. These strategies include policies and practices that had been in place prior to the Ph.D. Completion Project and those currently being implemented as part of the project. For many readers, it will be an exciting opportunity to survey a range of approaches to improving completion rates within U.S. doctoral programs and a chance to examine a new range of possibilities at their own universities. The culminating book in this project, scheduled for release in late 2010, will present a comprehensive analysis of all of the quantitative and qualitative data generated through the PhD. Completion Project, including a description of those interventions that appear to have a demonstrated effect on completion rates and attrition patterns over time.

ACKNOWLEDGMENTS

By Debra W. Stewart, President, Council of Graduate Schools

Many organizations and individuals deserve thanks for demonstrating ongoing commitments to this project, for supporting it financially, and for bringing it to fruition through their labors and their leadership. Let me begin with our funders. First we must thank Pfizer Inc, both for supporting the infrastructure for the Ph.D. Completion Project and for generously funding the fields of Science, Engineering, and Mathematics to bring about lasting impacts in these fields. From CGS's very first conversation with Pfizer about this project, Pfizer's divisions of Global Research and Development and Corporate Human Resources also expressed a deep commitment to developing the U.S. domestic talent pool and strengthening global research: the Ph.D. Completion Project would not exist without the leap of faith they took with CGS in the early days of this initiative. We also owe deep thanks to the Ford Foundation, whose strong support of Humanities and Social Sciences allowed us to expand the project to those important fields.

The proposal that CGS made to Pfizer and the Ford Foundation was based in part on the dialogue that occurred at an invitational workshop that CGS held in spring of 2003 with funding from the Alfred P. Sloan Foundation and the National Science Foundation. We would also like to express our appreciation to both the Sloan Foundation and NSF for their critical early support.

Of course, the Ph.D. Completion Project has also depended for its success on the member universities that constitute its core partners. We are grateful to all those who have informed and improved this project: the student respondents, the committed faculty, and the graduate deans and senior leaders in graduate education who have served as principal investigators or otherwise supported this important effort. To the Advisory Board members, listed in Appendix A, we thank you for your sound counsel, thoughtful selection of participants, willingness to provide periodic advice, and sustained commitment to reading drafts and offering comment as we published findings from the project. In particular, for their very careful reviews of this volume, we give our sincere thanks to Sheila Bonde, Dean of the Graduate School, Brown University; George Justice, Interim Vice Provost for Advanced Studies and Dean of the Graduate School, University of Missouri; Karen Klomparens, Dean of the Graduate School, Michigan State University; Nancy Marcus, Dean of the Graduate School, Florida State University; and William Weiner, Vice Provost for Research and Dean of the Graduate School, Marquette University.

Finally, I extend my personal thanks to the professional efforts of CGS staff (and friends) during all phases of this project. For their efforts at the formative stages of the project, I thank Joan Lorden, Les Sims, Carol Lynch, Robert Sowell, Jennifer Slimowitz, and Daniel Denecke, all of whom gave energetic efforts and thoughtful suggestions as we planned formal meetings and developed the proposal to our funders. For their contributions to the first phase of the project, I thank Daniel Denecke for his very important program direction and Helen Frasier and Matthew Loveless for their tireless efforts in data collection. And for their efforts during the current phase of the project, which has included data analysis, the drafting of publications, and continuing project leadership, I offer very special thanks to Robert Sowell, the director of the Ph.D. Completion Project, as well as to Nathan Bell, Sheila Kirby, Scott Naftel, Kenneth Redd, Ting Zhang, and Emily Neubig, who have provided their expertise in data collection and analysis; to Lewis Siegel for his especially helpful ongoing advice and counsel; and to Josh Mahler and Emily Esman for entering exit survey data. Like everything at CGS, the volumes emerging from this project are the result of a team effort. But it is only fair to recognize that it is the unique leadership of Robert Sowell and the special and determined labors of the Sowell, Bell, and Kirby team that have brought the current publication to fruition.

CHAPTER 1
Introduction

Background

In response to growing national concern about high levels of attrition from doctoral programs, the Council of Graduate Schools (CGS) launched the Ph.D. Completion Project in 2004 to examine and document attrition and completion patterns at a variety of universities, to encourage graduate schools and universities to develop and model intervention projects designed to both improve completion rates and reduce attrition, and to study and validate the impact of these interventions on Ph.D. completion. Early findings on completion rates–overall and disaggregated by student demographics–were reported in the first two publications of the project. A third report provided an overview of findings from exit surveys administered to Ph.D. completers on the factors that contributed to their ability to complete the doctoral degree and their experiences while in the program. This report–the fourth in the series reporting on data from the Ph.D. Completion Project–describes the interventions, policies, and practices implemented by the participating institutions to foster student success and reduce attrition. The remainder of this chapter provides an overview of the project and the first three reports in this series. The additional chapters in this monograph are described at the end of the chapter.

Project Overview

CGS initiated the Ph.D. Completion Project in 2004, with the generous support of Pfizer Inc and the Ford Foundation. The goal of the Ph.D. Completion Project was to identify strategies for positive change. In particular, the project sought to identify interventions that would increase Ph.D. completion rates of underrepresented minorities[1] in all fields, as well as the completion rates of women, especially in science, engineering and mathematics fields in which their overall completion rates are lower than those of men (Council of Graduate Schools, 2008b).

The project was funded in two phases. In Phase I (2004-2007) funding was provided to 21 major U.S. and Canadian universities. As Research Partners, these institutions provided baseline completion and attrition data and created and piloted interventions aimed at improving completion rates and reducing

---

1 Underrepresented minorities include U.S. citizen and permanent resident African Americans, Hispanics, and Native Americans.

attrition.[2] An additional 25 Project Partner universities–some of which provided data on completion and attrition–participated in various aspects of the project.[3] This pool of universities was expanded in Phase II (2007-2010) with additional funding from Pfizer Inc and the Ford Foundation. Twenty-one Research Partners, one Data Partner, and 21 Project Partners are included in Phase II (2007-2010). The wide range of universities, including private and public institutions, participating in the project was designed to ensure that the findings and practices that emerge would be applicable to the institutions producing the vast majority of Ph.D.s in the United States.

In Phase I, each Research Partner was required to provide program-level completion and attrition data for cohorts of students entering Ph.D. programs from 1992-93 through 2003-04. The institutions submitted data for a minimum of five programs in SEM (Science, Engineering, and Mathematics)[4] fields and a minimum of three in SSH (Social Sciences and Humanities) fields. Each institution was also required to submit baseline completion data by demographic characteristics (i.e., gender, citizenship and race/ethnicity for domestic students) for the same period and the same programs, but only at the broad field level (Engineering, Life Sciences, Mathematics & Physical Sciences, Social Sciences, and Humanities).

The project focused initially on completion rates for minorities because data from the U.S. Census Bureau suggest that the minority share of the college-age population will increase by 14% between 2007 and 2015, while the White, non-Hispanic college-age population will decrease by 6% in the same time period. Women were also a focus because although they make up one of the fastest growing segments of graduate student enrollment, their participation is overwhelmingly at the master's level and in non-SEM fields (Council of Graduate Schools, 2008b). Thus, to ensure a reasonable level of domestic production of Ph.D.s in SEM fields, the graduate community must address attrition of these groups first. We know that many of the policies, procedures, and practices that can be put in place to address attrition for these groups will increase completion for majority groups as well. Hence, the project considers all students, with special attention to minorities and women.

---

2 Baseline completion and attrition data from the one Canadian university participating as a Research Partner in Phase I of the Ph.D. Completion Project were used for analyses by program and gender, but not for analyses by citizenship and race/ethnicity, due to differing demographic definitions.

3 For a complete listing of Research Partners and Project Partners, see Appendix B.

4 We use the term "SEM" in this publication, rather than the more commonly used "STEM" (Science, Technology, Engineering, and Mathematics), because we group Social Sciences (which are typically included in the definition of STEM) with Humanities.

Overview of the Ph.D. Completion Project Publications

This section describes current and future publications that are intended to document the project. Findings from the first three reports in this series are briefly presented below.

In early 2008, CGS published *Ph.D. Completion and Attrition: Analysis of Baseline Program Data from the Ph.D. Completion Project* (Council of Graduate Schools, 2008a). The publication provided an overview of the Ph.D. Completion Project and focused on the baseline program completion and attrition data from 30 of the universities that provided data in Phase I of the project. The data were broken down by discipline, broad field, entering cohort size, and institution type (public or private). These data serve as a baseline from which to measure the impact of new policies, procedures, and practices designed to improve completion rates.

Data from Phase I of the project covered twelve academic years, 1992-93 through 2003-04. These data represent 330 programs and 49,113 students in 62 disciplines. For purposes of the analysis, students were divided into four groups–those who entered the doctoral program between 1992-93 and 1994-95 (A-Cohorts); those who entered between 1995-96 and 1997-98 (B-Cohorts); those who entered between 1998-99 and 2000-01 (C-Cohorts), and those who entered between 2001-02 and 2003-04 (D-Cohorts). Most of the analysis focused on ten-year completion rates of the A-Cohorts, although seven-year completion rates were also calculated for the A- and B-Cohorts. Early attrition was examined for the A-, B-, and C-Cohorts.

At the aggregate level, the data showed that 57% of the doctoral candidates in the sample completed their degree programs within a ten-year time span. However, Ph.D. completion rates varied by broad field, ranging from a high of 64% in Engineering to a low of 49% in Humanities. Within broad fields, completion rates varied widely across disciplines. For example, the cumulative ten-year completion rate in Computer and Information Sciences was about 41%, compared with 62% in Chemistry

The cumulative ten-year completion rate in all SEM fields combined was noticeably higher than in all SSH fields combined–59% versus 53%–but the combined SSH completion rate appeared to keep increasing after the ten-year mark. This finding suggests that a number of students in these broad fields will earn their degrees after ten years and that the differences in ultimate completion rates between broad fields may diminish.

The second publication in the series, *Ph.D. Completion and Attrition: Analysis of Baseline Demographic Data from the Ph.D. Completion Project* (Council of Graduate Schools, 2008b), focused on completion rates broken down by demographic characteristics (gender, citizenship, and race/ethnicity). It included an analysis of the demographic data submitted by 24 of the 30 universities that participated in Phase I of the project. The gender database included data for a total of 41,017 students at 24 institutions who started doctoral programs between 1992-93 and 2003-04. Of these students, 37% were female. The citizenship, race, and ethnicity database contained data for 39,758 students from 23 institutions (excluding the one Canadian institution). Of these students, 67% were domestic students who were distributed across U.S. racial/ethnic groups as follows: 6% African American, 9% Asian American, 4% Hispanic, 75% White, and 6% "Other." Because of their small numbers, Native American students were included in the last category.

The second report compared cumulative ten-year completion rates across demographic groups and across broad fields. Men, international students, and Whites had higher ten-year completion rates than women, domestic students, and students from other U.S. racial/ethnic groups, respectively. In the aggregate SEM fields men had higher completion rates than women while the opposite was true in the aggregate SSH fields. International students completed at higher rates than domestic students in both SEM and SSH fields and in all broad fields. Among domestic students, Whites had the highest completion rates in both SEM and SSH fields. African Americans had the highest completion rate in Humanities compared with other racial/ethnic groups and shared the highest completion rate in Life Sciences with White students. An important finding is that women and underrepresented minority students had higher late completion rates (from years eight through ten) than men and White students respectively.

The third report, *Ph.D. Completion and Attrition: Findings from Exit Surveys of Ph.D. Completers* (Council of Graduate Schools, 2009), reported on experiences and opinions of Ph.D completers who responded to an exit survey administered by 18 institutions participating in the Ph.D. Completion Project. Although the original intent had been to compare the experiences and opinions of completers and non-completers, the small number of non-completers who responded to the survey precluded such an analysis. A total of 1,406 Ph.D. completers responded to the exit survey between May 2006 and August 2008. The distribution of the completers across broad fields was as follows: Engineering – 16%, Life Sciences – 15%, Mathematics & Physical Sciences – 26%, Social Sciences – 21% and Humanities – 23%.

The major findings of the report included the following:

- Among major factors contributing to Ph.D. completion, financial support, mentoring/advising, and family support headed the list, with 80%, 65%, and 57% of respondents indicating that these were important. Compared with graduates from other fields, Humanities graduates were the least likely to cite financial support as a major factor in completion.
- Most students had access to an advisor, particularly during the final stages of the doctoral program. Humanities graduates were much less likely to report receiving regular feedback from their advisor or their program compared with those in SEM fields (78% versus 87-89%). Only 70% of Engineering graduates reported having access to a mentor compared with 77-81% of those in Life Sciences, Social Sciences, and Humanities. However, over 90% of all respondents indicated satisfaction with the quality of their relationship with their mentor and there was little difference by broad field of study.
- The overwhelming majority of respondents received financial support for their doctoral study (94%) and 70% reported that they were guaranteed multi-year support at the time of admission. Doctoral students in Mathematics & Physical Sciences appeared to have the most generous offers at time of admission, with 22% reporting that their offer included six or more years of guaranteed funding compared with only 2% of students in Social Sciences and 8% of those in Humanities. Among the respondents, Humanities students were the least likely to report being satisfied with the level of financial support during their program.
- Among those with teaching assistantships, there appeared to be considerable consensus that being a teaching assistant increased the length of the program, especially among Engineering and Life Sciences graduates. On the other hand, respondents were more mixed about the effect of research assistantships on length of time to degree completion.
- Over 80% of respondents reported that their graduate program sponsored events that allowed for informal conversations and interactions between faculty and students as well as among students. Only 45% of Life Sciences graduates reported that their program had a student lounge compared with 66-74% of graduates in other fields. While 91-94% of graduates in the Engineering and Mathematics & Physical Sciences fields reported that the program provided them with office space, this was true of only 71% of Humanities graduates and 66% of Life Sciences and Social Sciences graduates.
- Around 80 percent of those in the Engineering, Life Sciences, and Mathematics & Physical Sciences fields reported having research opportunities to prepare them for the dissertation phase compared with only 65% of Humanities graduates. The opportunity or ability to publish

one's own research while in the program was highest in the Engineering and Life Sciences fields and lowest in Humanities (87-92% versus 48%).

This monograph–the fourth publication in the series–reports on policies and practices at participating institutions that aim to improve Ph.D. completion rates and reduce attrition in doctoral programs. These policies and practices include both those that had been in place at these institutions prior to their participation in the Ph.D. Completion Project and those currently being implemented as part of the project. These policies and practices are categorized into six broad institutional and programmatic categories, using a framework outlined in a 2004 report by the Council of Graduate Schools (Council of Graduate Schools, 2004) for understanding the factors that influence Ph.D. completion or attrition. These include:

- Selection and admissions
- Mentoring and advising
- Financial support
- Research mode of the field
- Curricular and administrative processes and procedures
- Program environment

Although we categorize and discuss specific policies and practices under these broad headings, there is considerable overlap across the categories. Thus, a given intervention may well fit under two or more categories. For example, offering revised graduate student handbooks that make program requirements transparent would help students navigate the crucial early years of the doctoral program. We categorized this practice under improved "curricular and administrative processes and procedures," but it also speaks to "early advising" and, therefore, applies to "mentoring and advising" as well.

As the project continues and additional data are collected and analyzed, CGS will examine the impact of groups of interventions designed to improve completion rates. Many of the interventions are likely to affect completion and attrition only over the longer run and as such, sufficient time needs to elapse before we can evaluate their effectiveness. Some of these may prove to be most effective within specific fields and programs across most or all universities, whereas other interventions may work better in some institutional contexts than in others. While the project will probably be unable to isolate one strategy from all others as having a decisive effect on completion, there should be a demonstrable impact of groups of interventions on Ph.D. completion rates, and case studies will supplement the quantitative analysis.

The culminating publication in this series, scheduled for release in 2010, will include a comprehensive analysis of the quantitative and qualitative data submitted by the partnering universities in Phases I and II of the Ph.D. Completion Project, as well as a description of those policies and practices that appear to have had a demonstrated effect on completion rates and attrition patterns over time. It is our hope that the findings of the Ph.D. Completion Project will transform our understanding of the factors that contribute to higher Ph.D. completion rates nationwide, particularly for women and minorities.

Organization of the Report

Chapter 2 describes the process by which institutions were selected for participation in the Ph.D. Completion Project, including the criteria on which that selection was based, and summarizes the data and methods used in this report. Chapter 3 presents a brief profile of the participating institutions and their involvement in prior reform efforts aimed at revising and improving doctoral programs in general and supporting underrepresented students in particular. The chapter also discusses the broad goals that institutions hope to achieve by participation in the Ph.D. Completion project. Chapters 4-9 examine the range of interventions implemented by the institutions in support of their goals organized into the six different areas listed above: selection and admissions; mentoring and advising; financial support; research mode; curricular and administrative processes and procedures; and program environment. Each chapter describes the range of interventions adopted in that particular area across the range of institutions, using examples to illustrate specific interventions, as well as the progress on implementation. Space limitations precluded us from being able to describe the full set of interventions being implemented by the Research Partners. The examples provided are not meant to be exhaustive and do not imply that policies and practices of other institutions not highlighted were somehow less interesting or innovative. The goal was to be broadly representative of participating institutions and to illustrate the variety of interventions being implemented in a particular area. Chapter 10 previews the next steps for the Ph.D. Completion Project.

Appendix A lists the Ph.D. Completion Project Advisory Board members. Appendix B lists the Ph.D. Completion Project Research and Project Partners.

CHAPTER 2
Data and Methods

This report examines the set of interventions developed and implemented by institutions participating in the Ph.D. Completion Project. To provide some background, we first provide an overview of the proposal process through which institutions were selected to participate in the project and the reporting requirements attendant on selection. Understanding the selection process is important in that the institutional proposals, the pre-project assessments of interventions already in place that was required as a necessary part of participation, and the annual narrative reports required of participating institutions form the primary sources of data for this report.

The Ph.D. Completion Project consists of two phases: Phase I (2004-2007) and Phase II (2007-2010). Each had a proposal and selection process and while the majority of participating institutions selected in Phase I continued to participate in Phase II, there were a few that discontinued participation. In addition, a few institutions that had not been selected as Research Partners in Phase I but participated as unfunded partners in the project were funded to participate in Phase II. Because the ultimate objective of the project is to be able to document best practices in doctoral programs as evidenced by their effect in improving completion and reducing attrition, we need to be able to link data on interventions with completion and attrition data provided by the institutions. As a result, we focus here largely on the institutions that either participated in both Phases (the majority of institutions) or are current Phase II participants because we have current data on their programs, attrition, and completion rates that lend themselves to such an analysis. However, the description below necessarily encompasses both phases of the selection process.

The Selection Process

Phase I

In December 2003, with support from Pfizer Inc, CGS launched a major national initiative to address the issues of doctoral attrition and completion in the Science, Engineering, and Mathematics (SEM) disciplines. This was later expanded to the Social Sciences and Humanities (SSH) fields with support from the Ford Foundation. The ultimate intent of the project is to reduce rates of Ph.D. attrition and increase completion, as proven intervention strategies are widely disseminated and adopted by doctoral departments and programs. Special emphasis is directed to increasing completion rates for minority and women students.

To launch the Ph.D. Completion Project, CGS issued a request for proposals in June 2004 (Phase I), inviting its member institutions to apply for grants to create and pilot intervention strategies and to evaluate the effect of these strategies upon doctoral degree attrition patterns and completion rates. Institutions selected to participate in the initiative were to reflect a cross-section of both private and public universities that produce the bulk of Ph.D. graduates in SEM fields and SSH disciplines. Further, applicants had to demonstrate the capacity to collect completion and attrition data and use this data to benefit prospective students. Institutions were asked to define the doctoral attrition problem(s) for students–particularly minorities and women–that each program was trying to address and to articulate the specific sets of interventions that the institutions planned to implement to reduce attrition and increase completion within the specific institutional and program contexts. CGS listed several considerations that were to be given priority in the selection process: the scope of the applicants' doctoral programs; their past record of effecting change through systemic interventions; a demonstrated ability to collect relevant data; the quality of the proposed interventions; and evidence of the institution's commitment to sustaining project activity and evaluation beyond the three-year duration of the grant period. To ensure that the institutional leadership was fully engaged in the reform effort, all proposals had to demonstrate institutional commitment to the goals of the project through endorsement by senior administrative officials and concurrence of the project with institutional missions and strategic plans.

Specifically, to be eligible to apply, institutions had to:

- Propose to engage in activities to increase Ph.D. completion in a minimum of five programs drawn from the following broad SEM fields: physical sciences and mathematics, engineering and life sciences; and 3 programs drawn from the social sciences and humanities. Projects could select from a portfolio of optional policies and practices included as part of the RFP and/or propose other innovative practices not listed that they believed could contribute to a potential increase in Ph.D. completion rates. Priority consideration was to be given to institutions that proposed to implement at least 6 new interventions in at least 3 areas, linked to research findings in Ph.D. attrition and completion, that the institution believed would increase completion and that fell within the categories of improved selection processes; mentoring; financial support; processes and procedures; program environment; and research mode of field.
- Be able to present, at the time of application, Ph.D. program completion data for the programs selected for a recent 12-year period.
- Show evidence of prior institutionalization of a reform effort in graduate education, such as CGS's Preparing Future Faculty (PFF); the Carnegie Initiative on the Doctorate (CID); the Woodrow Wilson National

Fellowship Foundation's Responsive Ph.D.; NSF's Integrative Graduate Education and Research Traineeship (IGERT) and Alliance for Graduate Education and the Professoriate (AGEP); Mellon Foundation's Graduate Education Initiative.

- Demonstrate the commitment of the institution to the project including a graduate dean willing to take a leadership role, program directors willing to participate, and the support, evidenced by a letter of endorsement, of the university president or chief academic officer.

By the proposal deadline in November 2004, CGS received 45 proposals from 48 universities to participate in the Ph.D. Completion Project. Award recipients were selected by an external Advisory Board, appointed by CGS in June 2004 to guide the project. The Board was comprised of leaders from academia, industry, disciplinary societies, funding agencies, and research programs on minority graduate education. From a highly competitive pool of submitted proposals, CGS funded 18 proposals (including two joint, collaborative projects) submitted on behalf of 21 universities. A total of 239 departments/programs across these 21 universities agreed to participate in the project. Research Partners represent the demographic diversity of doctoral education in the U.S. and Canada; they include private and public universities from all regions of the U.S. and from Canada and minority-serving institutions.

Research Partners received awards of up to $100,000 over the 31-month grant period (November 2004-May 2007) to collect and submit data on doctoral completion and attrition; implement interventions in areas such as selection, mentoring, financial support, program environment, curricular processes, etc.; and develop rigorous assessment strategies to measure the impact of these interventions. Research Partners were required to submit annual narrative and financial reports to CGS.

The 21 Phase I Research Partners included:

Arizona State University
Cornell University
Duke University
Howard University
North Carolina State University
Princeton University
Purdue University
Université de Montréal (Canada)
University of California, Los Angeles
University of Cincinnati

University of Florida
University of Georgia
University of Illinois, Urbana-Champaign
University of Louisville
University of Maryland, Baltimore County
University of Michigan
University of Missouri–Columbia
University of Notre Dame
University of North Carolina at Chapel Hill
Washington University–St. Louis
Yale University

Because of the large number of strong proposals, and the overwhelming interest expressed by universities in working with CGS and its member institutions on issues of attrition and completion, CGS invited every institution that submitted a proposal to participate as a Project Partner, to submit data on completion and attrition, and to participate as fully as possible in the Ph.D. Completion Project. The incentive to participate was that all partners would have full access to information generated by the project as it developed and would meet semi-annually to share information and best practices with the broader graduate community. Eight Project Partner institutions became full participants and provided data on completion and attrition. Their inclusion along with the Research Partners in the Ph.D. Completion Project effort broadened the engagement of the community in Ph.D. completion, and thus, enhanced the impact of project outcomes.

Phase II

Recognizing that it was too early to discern the impact that the reforms implemented during Phase I had on completion rates and attrition patterns, CGS sought funding from both Pfizer Inc and Ford Foundation for a Phase II of the Ph.D. Completion Project that would run from 2007 through 2010. This longer time horizon would allow institutions to continue implementing the interventions and providing data on programs and completion rates and provide CGS with additional post-intervention data that could be used to examine the effect of interventions on completion and attrition rates.

In December 2006, CGS issued a request for proposals for Phase II, offering 31-month awards beginning May 1, 2007 to institutions that did not receive awards in Phase I (New Research Partners); institutions that had actively participated in Phase I as a Research Partner (Continuing Research Partners); and institutions that wished to submit completion and attrition data (Data-Only

Partners). The selection and eligibility criteria were the same as in Phase I with a few exceptions: Continuing Partners had to propose a plan for implementing mid-course corrections and enhancements of intervention strategies proposed during Phase I and New and Continuing Partners had to agree to convene graduate deans, staff, and department/program leaders at least once a year for an evidence-based discussion of completion rates and targets, the causes of doctoral attrition, and strategies for enhancing Ph.D. completion. Once again, Research Partners were required to provide annual reports to CGS.

Seven new Research Partners joined the Ph.D. Completion Project in Phase II–three new institutions and four former Project Partners, who had been very active in developing and implementing interventions in Phase I. The 21 Phase II Research Partners includes the following (new Research Partners are in italics):

Brown University
Cornell University
Duke University
Howard University
Florida State University
Marquette University
Michigan State University
North Carolina State University
Ohio State University
Pennsylvania State University
Purdue University
University of California, Los Angeles
University of California, San Diego
University of Cincinnati
University of Georgia
University of Illinois, Urbana-Champaign
University of Maryland, Baltimore County
University of Michigan
University of Missouri–Columbia
University of North Carolina at Chapel Hill
Yale University

There is also one funded Data Partner–University of Southern California–that provides data on completion and attrition but is not required to adopt interventions or report on the progress or effects of implementing these interventions.

Six Phase I Research Partners became Project Partners in Phase II. These included:

Arizona State University
Princeton University
University of Florida
University of Louisville
University of Notre Dame
Washington University in St. Louis

As mentioned above, we focus on institutions participating as Research Partners in Phase II because we want to be able to examine the relationship between the interventions and doctoral completion and attrition. We have consistent and long-term data only for institutions who are currently active participants in the project (Phase II Research Partners). Table 2.1 presents the complete list of the 21 Research Partners and 250 programs by broad field that are participating in Phase II of the Ph.D. Completion Project. Overall, 157 SEM and 93 Humanities and Social Sciences departments/programs are participating in the project. The Mathematics & Physical Sciences field accounts for about one-quarter (24.8%) of all participating programs; Engineering for about one-fifth (19.7%); Life Sciences and Humanities 18.7% each; and Social Sciences 17.7%.

Data Sources and Methods

The data sources for this report include the following:

1. Institutional proposals submitted in response to CGS's RFPs: For the majority of institutions, we have both Phase I and Phase II proposals. These proposals provide a wealth of detail about the project as envisioned by each institution: the goals of the project; prior involvement in other efforts aimed at improving outcomes for doctoral students; the number of participating departments/programs and why they were selected to participate in the project; the types of intervention proposed by the institution and the rationale for why these were chosen; and evidence of commitment of top-level leaders to the project.

2. Two baseline assessment templates created by CGS, one for departments and/or program activities and resources, and another for institution-level activities and resources: Institutions and programs were requested to submit baseline information about the effectiveness and duration of policies, practices, and programs that were already in place prior to the implementation of activities supported by the Ph.D. Completion Project.

13

Table 2.1. Research Partners and Participating Programs, by Broad Field

Research Partner	Institution	Engineering	Life Sciences	Mathematics & Physical Sciences	Social Sciences	Humanities	Total Number of Participating Programs
Phase II	Brown University	1	1	2	2	2	8
Phase I & II	Cornell University	1	2	2	2	3	10
Phase I & II	Duke University	2	1	3	1	3	10
Phase II	Florida State University	0	1	4	1	2	8
Phase I & II	Howard University	1	1	3	2	1	8
Phase II	Marquette University	4	2	2	2	4	14
Phase II	Michigan State University	1	5	1	1	3	11
Phase I & II	North Carolina State University	2	3	4	3	0	12
Phase II	Ohio State University	1	2	2	2	2	9
Phase I & II	Pennsylvania State University	4	0	3	3	1	11
Phase I & II	Purdue University	4	1	3	3	3	14
Phase I & II	University of California, Los Angeles	2	2	2	4	9	19
Phase II	University of California, San Diego	2	1	2	2	1	8
Phase I & II	University of Cincinnati	10	6	0	2	1	19
Phase I & II	University of Georgia	0	3	4	3	2	12
Phase I & II	University of Illinois, Urbana–Champaign	3	3	4	2	2	14
Phase I & II	University of Maryland, Baltimore County	5	4	10	4	1	24
Phase I & II	University of Michigan	3	1	1	1	2	8
Phase I & II	University of Missouri–Columbia	1	5	2	2	2	12
Phase I & II	University of North Carolina at Chapel Hill	2	0	5	1	2	10
Phase I & II	Yale University	1	2	2	2	2	9
Total Number of Programs by Broad Field		50	46	61	46	47	250

Consistent with the goals of the Ph.D. Completion Project, these tools were designed to assess existing interventions across each of the major points of the doctoral career and each of the six areas of institutional factors known to contribute to attrition: selection and admissions; mentoring and advising; financial support; research mode of the field; curricular processes and procedures; and program environment.

3. The Ph.D. Completion Project website (www.phdcompletion.org), launched on July 2, 2004, contains an overview of the project and brief profiles of each participating institution including an abstract of the project, participating programs, and interventions implemented by the institution. The website also includes a promising practices section which lists policies and practices identified by the institutions as promising in the six areas listed above.

4. Annual narrative reports provided by the institutions to CGS. These described progress in implementing the interventions, successes and challenges in implementation, and qualitative evidence of the impact of the project on the institution, departments, faculty, and students. In Phase II, institutions were also asked to respond to a series of general questions:

A) During Phase II, how has the graduate school used attrition and completion data collected as a result of this project?

B) Have attrition and completion data been integrated into formal processes in the university as a result of this project? If so, how?

C) What evidence do you have of changes in faculty perception or understanding of attrition and completion in participating programs changed as a result of this project?

D) What impact have project activities had to-date on women and students from underrepresented minority groups (including minority women)? On doctoral students in participating program overall?

5. Notes from site visits to a number of the participating institutions by CGS staff: CGS staff conducted one-day site visits where they met with the graduate deans, department chairs, faculty and students to ask about the project and project-sponsored activities, issues related to doctoral degree attrition, and what else could be done to enhance the participants' abilities to meet their goals for improving completion rates, especially for students from underrepresented groups. Notes from these site visits were a useful supplement to the annual reports filed by the institutions.

To build profiles of the institutions, we asked them to provide data on selected characteristics of the institution and student body, using a common template and for a defined point in time.

To understand what was already in place at the institutions, we used the pre-project assessment forms submitted by the institutions in either 2005 or 2007 that asked institutions to check off existing policies and practices along with how long each practice or policy had been in place: 0-2 years; 3-5 years; 6-9 years, and 10+ years. The two assessment forms had some differences in the list of policies and practices about which institutions were asked based on information collected during Phase I. One major change was the deletion of the "current effectiveness" rating from the Phase II template, because these ratings appeared to be more subjective than evidence-based. As a result, we do not report on these here. Of the 21 Research Partners, 14 submitted pre-project/factor assessments in either 2005 or 2007, so the extant practices discussed in this monograph are necessarily incomplete.

To facilitate analysis, we first combined the data from the proposals and the annual reports into spreadsheets that focused on different themes–goals of the project; involvement in prior reform efforts; proposed interventions and rationale; implementation progress, successes, and challenges; and evidence of impact of the project on fostering a culture of evidence, on faculty perceptions and behavior, and on doctoral students, in particular, students from underrepresented groups. These spreadsheets allowed us to examine common themes across the set of institutions within these broad topics.

To analyze the types of interventions, we coded them into the six separate "bins" or areas listed previously and then coded them in two ways. First, for each area, we developed a comprehensive list of policies and practices that were proposed by the institutions. This gave us a detailed list of proposed specific interventions within each area. Second, for some of the areas, it seemed useful to code the detailed list of interventions into somewhat broader subcategories. Thus, for example, we examined the detailed set of interventions proposed or implemented under mentoring and advising by all the Research Partners and then grouped them into subgroups such as "annual student assessments of progress;" "resources for students to develop productive mentoring relationships; "resources for faculty to provide effective mentoring" etc. This allowed us to highlight examples of interventions in these subgroups that seemed promising or interesting or a particularly good example of a particular intervention. We remind the reader that these lists are not meant to be exhaustive and that, while we identify these practices as "promising," we do not–as yet–have rigorous evidence of their effectiveness. Nonetheless, the set of practices highlighted in this monograph appear to have the potential of successfully addressing several areas of concern in doctoral education. Thus, they may be of interest to the larger community of doctoral institutions facing similar issues.

In selecting examples to highlight, we tried to be inclusive of all Research Partners and to be broadly representative and illustrative; thus, our choices do not represent a ranking or judgment that policies and practices of other institutions not highlighted were somehow less interesting or innovative. Because of space limitations, we limited the number of examples taken from each institution to four across the various substantive chapters. The highlights are taken verbatim from institutions' proposals, annual reports, and occasionally from the CGS site visit reports. We use text boxes to distinguish these quotations from the more general discussion. Each quotation is preceded by the name of the institution in italics. In a few instances, where particular programs were not fully described in the proposals or annual reports, we used material from institutional websites to supplement the description.

The next chapter provides a brief overview of the Research Partners participating in Phase II and their prior involvement in efforts to reform doctoral education and improve student outcomes.

CHAPTER 3
Profile of Participating Institutions

This chapter provides a summary profile of the Phase II Research Partners in terms of selected characteristics, prior involvement in doctoral education reform, and goals they hoped to achieve by participating in the Ph.D. Completion Project. Overall, this sample includes typical major public and private institutions, geographically dispersed institutions, and both large and small institutions, as shown in Table 3.1. The characteristics shown in this table are as of Fall 2008.

Six out of 21 Research Partners in Phase II of the project are private institutions and the remaining 15 are public institutions. All are Research Universities–18 are classified as "very high research activity" and the remaining three are "high research activity" universities under the Carnegie classification. These institutions are drawn from all four Census regions–West, Midwest, Northeast, and South. The total number of doctoral programs offered by these universities ranges from 21 (Marquette University) to 138 (Michigan State University). The total number of graduate students enrolled at these universities ranged from approximately 1,000 (Howard University) to over 10,000 (Michigan State University; Ohio State University; University of Illinois, Urbana–Champaign). The number enrolled in doctoral programs ranged from under 1,000 to over 5,000 students. Marquette University had the smallest number of doctoral students in 2008 (n=536) while the University of Illinois, Urbana–Champaign had the largest number (n=5,091).

The percentage of women doctoral students ranged from 40% (Purdue University; University of California, San Diego) to 63% (Howard University). The majority of institutions (17 out of 21) reported that the percentage of U.S. minority students enrolled in doctoral programs was less than 20%. Howard University was again the exception–86% of its doctoral students were U.S. minority. The percentage of international students enrolled in doctoral programs ranged from 14% (Howard University) to 50% (Purdue University).

Previous Initiatives to Reform Doctoral Education

The RFPs issued by CGS asked institutions to describe their prior and current involvement in efforts to reform doctoral education. Institutions described two kinds of efforts–involvement in national initiatives to reform the nature of doctoral education and participation in a number of fellowship and traineeships aimed largely at underrepresented groups of students. Because

Table 3.1. Profile of Phase II Research Partners

Name of Institution	Type of Institution (Public, Private)	Carnegie Classification*	Number of Doctoral Programs	Number of Graduate Students		Percentage Women	Of Doctoral Students:	
				Total	Enrolled in Doctoral Programs		Percentage U.S. Minority	Percentage International Students
Brown University	Private	RU/VH	46	1,808	1,333	46%	12%	38%
Cornell University	Private	RU/VH	83	4,835	3,197	42%	11%	41%
Duke University	Private	RU/VH	45	4,132	2,195	46%	13%	33%
Florida State University	Public	RU/VH	78	8,370	2,597	48%	15%	25%
Howard University	Private	RU/H	28	1,081	715	63%	86%	14%
Marquette University	Private	RU/H	21	2,423	536	48%	26%	20%
Michigan State University	Public	RU/VH	138	10,311	3,324	49%	11%	42%
North Carolina State University	Public	RU/VH	62	6,931	2,859	42%	11%	37%
Ohio State University	Public	RU/VH	98	10,219	4,935	51%	10%	35%
Pennsylvania State University	Public	RU/VH	120	9,206	4,328	45%	8%	42%
Purdue University	Public	RU/VH	58	7,427	4,179	40%	8%	50%
University of California, Los Angeles	Public	RU/VH	82	9,747	4,714	47%	25%	23%
University of California, San Diego	Public	RU/VH	42	4,264	2,886	40%	9%	23%
University of Cincinnati	Public	RU/VH	82	7,715	2,484	52%	9%	32%
University of Georgia	Public	RU/VH	102	7,160	2,643	54%	21%	28%
University of Illinois, Urbana–Champaign	Public	RU/VH	95	10,065	5,091	41%	8%	46%
University of Maryland, Baltimore County	Public	RU/H	24	2,656	746	50%	16%	32%
University of Michigan	Public	RU/VH	104	7,229	4,668	44%	16%	35%
University of Missouri–Columbia	Public	RU/VH	71	6,028	2,132	49%	13%	30%
University of North Carolina at Chapel Hill	Public	RU/VH	66	6,925	3,419	56%	17%	19%
Yale University	Private	RU/VH	54	2,663	2,436	48%	13%	30%

*RU/VH: Research Universities (very high research activity); RU/H: Research Universities (high research activity) not all institutions listed all the initiatives with which they had been previously or currently involved, we provide broad estimates of the numbers involved in each initiative rather than exact counts.

National Initiatives to Reform Doctoral Education

These included the following:

The Pew Charitable Trust's Re-envisioning the Ph.D. Project

Two institutions participated in the Pew Charitable Trusts Re-envisioning the Ph.D. project, which identified and provided examples of attempts to redesign doctoral education; explored the connections among the efforts, issues, and stakeholders involved; developed a set of strategies to effect change; and served as a clearinghouse of innovative practices in doctoral education. The Re-envisioning the Ph.D. project ended in June 2003, but the University of Washington Graduate School continues to maintain a project website (http://www.grad.washington.edu/envision/index.html).

Carnegie Initiative on the Doctorate (CID)

About two-fifths of the institutions were involved in the CID, which launched in 2002 with the goal of improving the education of doctoral students. A total of 44 universities and 84 departments of chemistry, education, English, history, mathematics, and neuroscience participated in the project (http://www.carnegiefoundation.org/programs/index.asp?key=29). Participating departments engaged in a process of reflection, implementation of program changes, and assessment to strengthen doctoral programs at their institutions. The CID also commissioned essays on the future of doctoral education in each of the six disciplines, and a final volume, *The Formation of Scholars: Rethinking Doctoral Education for the Twenty-First Century*, published in 2008, presents the lessons learned from the project.

Woodrow Wilson National Fellowship Foundation's Responsive Ph.D. Initiative

Six institutions participated in the Responsive Ph.D. initiative launched by the Woodrow Wilson National Fellowship Foundation in 2000 to examine the mismatch between the training doctoral students receive in graduate school and the careers available to them (http://www.woodrow.org/policy/responsivephd/index.php). Four central principles guided the project: the Ph.D. degree requires strong graduate schools and graduate deans with real budgets and real scope; doctoral education benefits from a continuing dialogue with the worlds beyond academia; doctoral education should reflect the diversity of the U.S.

population; and the quality of doctoral education depends on evaluation and assessment. The project concluded in 2006.

Andrew Mellon Foundation's Graduate Education Initiative (GEI)

A small number of the institutions participated in the GEI, initiated by the Andrew W. Mellon Foundation in 1991, to improve the quality of graduate programs in the humanities and social sciences, reduce attrition, and shorten the time-to-degree (http://www.mellon.org). Over a 10-year period, the Foundation provided $58 million to 54 departments in the humanities and related social sciences at 10 major research universities. These departments were encouraged to review their curricula, examinations, advising, official timetables, and dissertation requirements with an eye to facilitating timely degree completion and to reducing attrition while maintaining or increasing the quality of doctoral training they provided. In the process, systematic data were assembled on students' progress–or lack of it–thus providing participating departments and institutions with information needed to track the effectiveness of their efforts.

Preparing Future Faculty (PFF)

The majority of institutions were participating in CGS's PFF program. This is a national movement to transform the way aspiring faculty members are prepared for their careers (http://www.preparing-faculty.org). PFF programs provide doctoral students, as well as some master's students and postdoctorates, with opportunities to observe and experience faculty responsibilities at a variety of academic institutions with varying missions, diverse student bodies, and different expectations for faculty. The PFF initiative was launched in 1993 as a partnership between the Council of Graduate Schools and the American Association of Colleges and Universities (AAC&U). From 1993 to 2003, PFF programs were implemented at more than 45 doctoral degree-granting institutions and nearly 300 partner institutions in the United States.

Center for the Integration of Research, Teaching, and Learning (CIRTL)

At least a third of the institutions indicated some degree of involvement with CIRTL and some were actively engaged in applying CIRTL interventions. The Center aims to develop a national faculty in science, technology, engineering, and mathematics (STEM) committed to implementing and advancing effective teaching practices for diverse student audiences (http://www.cirtl.net/). CIRTL promotes best practices in STEM teaching and learning and creates learning communities to support and sustain the improvement of teaching and learning practice.

Fellowship and Traineeship Programs

A number of institutions were participating in several fellowship and training programs, primarily funded by the National Science Foundation (NSF) and the U.S. Department of Education.

Ns#### National Science Foundation Programs

About two-thirds of the institutions were participating in NSF's Alliance for Graduate Education and the Professoriate (AGEP) program and/or the Integrative Graduate Education and Research Traineeship (IGERT) program. The AGEP program seeks to increase the number of U.S. citizens and permanent residents receiving doctoral degrees and entering the professoriate in STEM, with special emphasis on underrepresented minorities (http://www. agep.us/). Partnering institutions work to enhance the recruitment, mentoring, and retention of minority students in STEM doctoral programs, and to develop strategies to identify and support underrepresented minorities who want to pursue academic careers. The IGERT program provides interdisciplinary training, combined with deep disciplinary knowledge, to doctoral students in STEM (http://www.igert.org/). The program seeks to transcend traditional disciplinary boundaries and provide students with the tools to become the future leaders in science and engineering. Since 1998, the IGERT program has provided funding to nearly 5,000 graduate students in over 100 universities in 41 states, the District of Columbia, and Puerto Rico. Other NSF programs that were mentioned in the proposals included Vertical Integration of Research and Education (VIGRE); ADVANCE Institutional Transformation Award; Bridge to the Doctorate programs; and the Louis Stokes Alliances for Minority Participation (LSAMP) program.

Department of Education Program

Another program that was mentioned by a number of institutions was the U.S. Department of Education's Graduate Assistant in Areas of National Need (GAANN) Fellowship program. This program provides fellowships, through academic departments and programs of institutions of higher education, to assist graduate students with excellent records who demonstrate financial need and plan to pursue the highest degree available in their course study at the institution in a field designated as an area of national need. The goals of the program are to increase the percentage of GAANN fellows who obtain a doctorate degree in an area of national need; to increase the percentage of GAANN fellows from traditionally underrepresented populations; and to decrease the time-to-degree for GAANN fellows receiving Ph.D.s.

In the remainder of this chapter and in subsequent chapters, we provide selected illustrations of goals and interventions taken verbatim from the proposals and annual reports of the institutions. As noted earlier, these quotations are in text boxes, with names of institutions in italics.

Goals of the Research Partners

The ultimate intent of the Ph.D. Completion Project is to reduce rates of Ph.D. attrition and increase completion rates, particularly among underrepresented minorities and women, by highlighting and disseminating promising institutional policies and practices. Following CGS, all the institutions set as the overall goal for their project a reduced attrition rate and improved completion rate in the doctoral programs participating in the project, with a special emphasis on improved outcomes of underrepresented minority and women students. Starting with the participating programs, most institutions expected the lessons learned to be useful in reducing attrition and increasing completion rates across the board.

One collaborative proposal described four conditions for student success that were the target of their interventions:

> *University of Georgia/North Carolina State University/University of Florida*:
>
> Condition #1: The right people apply for doctoral study
>
> Condition #2: The right applicants are admitted as doctoral students
>
> Condition #3: Students and faculty form productive working relationships
>
> Condition #4: Students experience social support from fellow students.

Some institutions were more specific with respect to desired reductions in attrition or improvement in completion rates. For example:

> *Cornell University:* Our goal is to improve completion rates in those fields that are below average for their disciplinary area, as well as to improve completion rates for student groups that currently complete at below-average rates. Eventually, we would like to see completion rates of all student groups in all disciplines approach those in the best biological and physical science fields.
>
> *Duke University:* We would like, as a Graduate School, to see our overall completion rates come closer to 75% than the current 64%.
>
> *University of Cincinnati:* Specific goals for appropriate Ph.D. completion percentages are…presently premature. Nevertheless, a completion percentage of 50% is clearly unacceptable. A goal of 75% is our stretch goal, certainly

attainable in several of our 20 programs; a firm goal of increasing the completion rate by 10% in each program is within our grasp.

University of Michigan: We would like to increase completion, first by reducing late attrition, and second by reducing early attrition (i.e. first or second years) which is currently about 25%. We believe we will be able to identify and target vulnerable populations who are most likely to leave without a degree. We also would like to target completion within 7 years as often as possible.

Yale University: A 10% increase in student retention for each of the nine programs. Female and underrepresented minority (URM) students will complete their programs at a minimum at the same rate as all others in their department.

In addition, Cornell–which has a large number of international students–highlighted the need to pay attention to these students and the challenges they face:

Cornell University: In addition to the minority student populations mentioned above, we plan to pay particular attention to international students… International students may face additional concerns with funding, language, culture, and other factors that significantly impact their graduate experience and that set them apart from domestic students. Such factors may further complicate the considerations of ethnicity and gender of particular concern in this CGS endeavor.

We now turn to a description of interventions implemented by the Research Partners grouped under the six areas identified earlier:

- Selection and admissions
- Mentoring and advising
- Financial support
- Research mode of the field
- Curricular processes and procedures
- Program environment.

For each area, we briefly describe the range of promising policies and practices implemented by the institutions and provide some examples to illustrate. In many cases, institutions already had a number of these policies and practices in place prior to the CGS project as evidenced by their pre-project/factor assessment forms and we note that in the discussion.

CHAPTER 4
Promising Practices: Student Selection and Admissions

For most universities, the opportunity to increase the rate of student success in Ph.D. programs begins with the recruitment and selection processes for admissions. Recruiting for success means drawing in talented students from diverse backgrounds who have the potential to succeed in a program of their chosen discipline. But it also means identifying and attracting those who are likely to thrive within a specific departmental culture, university environment, and surrounding locale.

One important aspect of recruiting and selecting students is looking for those whose prior experience suggests an ability to succeed in academic coursework, which typically constitutes the first years of doctoral study. Common admissions materials (including test scores and transcripts of undergraduate performance) tend to be good predictors of early success in graduate school. But selecting students for doctoral programs often also depends upon identifying those who have demonstrated the potential to succeed in the later years of a Ph.D., when what is required may be creativity, ability to work in collaborative research settings, and/or perseverance in pursuing independent lines of inquiry that will result in an acceptable dissertation. Early predictors of success in the later stages of doctoral work, particularly in the dissertation stage, are more difficult to define, and require careful review and deliberation by the admissions committee.

Universities participating in the Ph.D. Completion Project use a variety of mechanisms for integrating into the doctoral admissions process a greater attention to the "fit" or "match" between a particular student and a specific program, alongside considerations of traditional measures of student quality. These mechanisms may include the provision of greater transparency about expectations and outcomes, more opportunities for students to visit campus before admission or enrollment, and more intensive orientation once students arrive on campus. A consistent theme across each of these areas of intervention in selection process for admissions is the recruitment, retention and success of underrepresented students. The recognition of the crucial role of active recruitment–especially of women and minorities–was shared by many institutions.

Many of these policies and practices were already extant at the universities. For example, in their pre-project assessments, universities reported a total of over 70 existing policies, practices and programs, many of which mirror the ones above. Most of these had been in place for 10 or more years. The most commonly reported were 'pre-admission visits to campus' and 'selection criteria in addition to GPA and GRE scores employed.' The least commonly-reported practice was 'completion data provided for prospective students,' reported by just over a third of the universities and fairly recently implemented.

In this and subsequent chapters, we list promising practices in each broad area and then provide additional details by highlighting selected practices through illustrative examples. As mentioned earlier, the list is not meant to be exhaustive and, while we identify these practices as "promising," we do not–as yet–have evidence of their effectiveness. Nonetheless, the practices listed here and in following chapters are promising in that they have the potential of addressing areas of concern in doctoral education, and, as such, of relevance to the larger community of doctoral institutions.

Promising Practices

We categorized promising practices identified by participating universities in the area of selection and admissions under broad headings but these are not mutually exclusive categories and there is considerable overlap among them. Promising practices include:

Recruitment

- Offer pre-admission and pre-enrollment campus visits:
    - o Expand the opportunities for departments to bring prospective students to campus for recruitment visits, with emphasis on those students from underrepresented populations
    - o Reimburse direct expenses related to group campus visits
- Use early research opportunities as a recruitment tool:
    - o Identify top undergraduates and invite them to participate in a research institute late in their sophomore year to prepare and recruit these students to pursue doctoral studies [See also 'Research Experience']
    - o Summer Pre-Doctoral Institute for underrepresented students
- Improve efforts to recruit underrepresented students:
    - o Appoint new Diversity Coordinator to devote year-round efforts to minority recruiting
    - o Increase departmental participation in the Diversity Outreach Collaboration and the Diversity Coordinators Project to produce a diverse applicant pool for each department/program
    - o Send staff, faculty, and/or student teams to recruitment fairs across the country, as well as to HBCUs and other top universities

- o Attend national conferences that feature undergraduate research, and provide professional development and mentoring activities for underrepresented students
- o Publish email directory of summer research programs, and build strong working relationships with faculty across the country
- o Create pipelines to the university through the Ronald McNair Scholars Program, McNair Summer Research Conference, multicultural directors from the three colleges, and the Women in Science and Engineering (WISE) Program, and other sources
- o Incorporate alumni into program recruitment strategies, in particular women and members of underrepresented groups who graduated after 1975
- o Develop comprehensive university-wide plan for recruiting and retaining students from underrepresented populations and/or women

Transparency

- Improve department websites to ensure that each includes additional data, information, and resources necessary for prospective students to make informed decisions.
- Increase transparency in the selection processes and clarify expectations for students in their doctoral programs, including assessment milestones

Admissions

- Develop workshops for admissions committees and program chairs and informational workshops on diversity for faculty involved in graduate admissions
- Select students based on "fit" to program goals and faculty research expertise
- Develop a post-admissions grid that describes each newly admitted student according to a set of criteria pertinent to graduate school persistence including four common elements across all programs and up to two program-specific predictors
- Create protocol, through data gathered in exit survey, to help identify candidates who are committed to the Ph.D. career path
- Survey applicants to determine why admissions offers are accepted or declined; compare with exit data

Selected Highlights

As mentioned earlier, space limitations preclude us from describing the full set of interventions in each area across all institutions. Thus, we focus on a few types of interventions and then within that type, we select up to six examples to highlight. Our choices do not imply that the practice did not exist at other universities or that the policies and practices implemented by other institutions not highlighted were somehow less interesting or innovative. In each case, we identify the institution and provide a description of the intervention taken verbatim from the proposals or annual reports.

Offer pre-admission and pre-enrollment campus visits

University of Cincinnati: The Graduate Recruitment Weekend…offers an excellent opportunity to study the efficacy of on-campus visits and interaction between prospective students, faculty, and current students, thereby facilitating the appropriateness of program-student matches. Post-event surveys of student participants in recent years indicate that over 96% found the Recruitment Weekend to be helpful or very helpful in their graduate school decision-making process. The Recruitment Weekend has been an effective tool for attracting top students to the University of Cincinnati with greater than 50% of the event participants matriculating.

University of North Carolina at Chapel Hill: Campus visits–either within a structured summer research program or as briefer pre-enrollment visits–can encourage student interest by revealing the program's commitment to student success through the accomplishments of their enrolled students. Campus visits also provide opportunities for interaction with relevant role models. From the departmental perspective, it provides information about student interests that cannot be gleaned from the traditional application… Thirty-four percent of the students who were offered travel awards (CGS funds) to visit the UNC-Chapel Hill campus spring 2006 have entered a graduate program in one of our eleven selected departments included in this study. Sixty-seven percent of these students were female and fifty percent were underrepresented minorities. Departments attribute their success in recruiting these students in part to the increased contact with appropriate role models and one-on-one time afforded by the on-campus visits.

Use early research opportunities as a recruitment tool

Duke University: [The] Office of Graduate Student Affairs (GSA) directs the Summer Research Opportunities Program (SROP) and Post-baccalaureate Research Education Program (PREP) for minority students. The success of these programs has already been shown in that past SROP fellows have entered strong graduate programs at universities such as Duke, University of Michigan, University of Chicago, Johns Hopkins, and Case Western Reserve University… Thirteen of our past SROP Fellows are enrolled at Duke for graduate studies.

University of Illinois at Urbana-Champaign: offers a summer research program that provides undergraduate students from populations underrepresented in graduate study at Illinois with an opportunity to explore careers in research… The many activities offered through the Summer Research Opportunities Program afford participants an opportunity to establish important relationships with faculty in their respective fields of study, conduct graduate-level research under the supervision of a University of Illinois renowned faculty member, become acquainted with the culture of graduate school, and to learn what is needed and expected of them as graduate students in their discipline at the University of Illinois (http://www.grad.illinois.edu/eep/srop/)

Improve efforts to recruit underrepresented students

Ohio State University: [To increase the number of women in Physics, the department plans to] [d]evelop a new recruiting strategy by surveying our current students, both graduate and undergraduate, in an effort to uncover the key factors limiting their recruitment of women. We will request additional input from the [Committee on the Status of Women in Physics]… During the 2007-08 academic year, Physics sponsored four recruiting trips for female prospective graduate students. From that candidate pool, eight women graduate students enrolled in the Physics doctoral program beginning Autumn 2008.

Pennsylvania State University: In partnership with the Ronald McNair Scholars Program and Summer Research Opportunity Program (SROP), operated in conjunction with other CIC institutions, the Graduate School and the ten programs will identify and cultivate potential recruits in their junior years. Institutions that historically have been pipelines for these programs will be prime targets for these recruiting efforts and new pipelines will be fostered with other institutions… Penn State sponsors a McNair Summer Research Conference, annually hosting approximately 300 to 400 McNair scholars from around the United States. This conference provides a unique opportunity to introduce the young scholars to faculty and graduate students from the participating programs. The Graduate School will sponsor a roundtable reception during this annual conference to enable students and faculty from the ten doctoral programs to develop contacts with the McNair Scholars. Follow up communications with prospects identified at this summer event will be made by the graduate officers, program faculty, students, and alumni from the programs… Other prospects will be identified by the multi-cultural directors from each of the three colleges and the Women in Science and Engineering

Program (WISE). The multicultural directors have extensive contacts with programs at HBCUs to identify potential graduate student recruits for the participating programs. The science and engineering faculty participate in the WISE program. Through these connections, ties will be established with women's colleges in the United States for the expressed purpose of recruiting women to the ten programs… All programs also will incorporate alumni into their recruitment strategies, in particular women and members of underrepresented groups who graduated after 1975.

University of Maryland, Baltimore County: One of the major initiatives of the PROMISE program is an event called Graduate Horizons where 100 students from around the country are brought to UMBC for a weekend to learn about graduate education and general and opportunities at UMBC in particular. The goal is to increase enrollment of underrepresented minority students, however, participation in this program is open to all domestic students. The PROMISE program provides funds to bring students to campus who were not able to visit during the Graduate Horizons weekend. Some of these students are identified by the PROMISE program while others are in direct contact with the departments.

Yale University: [Under the Diversity Recruitment Program] a faculty member within each department has been appointed as a diversity coordinator (DC)…(who) will play a critical role in the development, implementation, and evaluation of departmental- and/or program-specific minority student recruitment activities during the academic year. Specifically, the DC will a) be an active member of the department admissions committee and will serve as an advocate for students of diverse backgrounds; b) serve as a resource for prospective applicants from diverse backgrounds; c) work closely with the Assistant Dean for Diversity to identify potential feeder schools thereby identifying outstanding diverse student applicants early in the process; d) coordinate travel to feeder schools and provide timely correspondence to diverse applicants throughout the admissions process; e) conduct phone interviews with diverse applicants as appropriate; f) encourage admitted diverse applicants to attend Diversity Recruitment Days; g) provide a short summary report to the Dean of the Graduate School on the general outcome of the diversity recruitment process at the end of each admissions cycle.

Improve department websites

University of California, San Diego: Create web based information on the home pages of the eight target departments that provides program completion data, selection criteria, program information and requirements for each area of study, a list of all faculty with research areas, links to faculty web sites and research centers that provide opportunities for student involvement, financial support information, campus housing information, and department and campus student organization information.

University of Illinois, Urbana–Champaign: The Graduate Program Profiles Project began with the vision of having an online single-page snapshot of summary data for each graduate program at the University of Illinois. This one-page summary would provide an administrative overview of each program and speak to the quality of the program… We envision that the inclusion of the following types of program information: 10+ years of application, admissions, new enrollment, enrollment, and degree counts and trends, with these data items further divided by race/ethnic, gender, citizenship, and residency; degree completion; time to degree; sources and levels of support including assistantships and fellowships; contact information.

Select students based on "fit" to program goals and faculty research expertise

Howard University: In the area of graduate student recruitment, in an effort to build upon the notion of determining a "good program fit" during the admissions review; faculty in Phase II will be engaged in the process of identifying top undergraduate students from Howard University exhibiting a commitment to research pursuits. Those students identified late in their sophomore year will begin an undergraduate research internship designed to prepare them to pursue doctoral studies at Howard. The internship experience will expose these undergraduate scholars to faculty expectations of graduate student work and graduate student mentors with the underlying purpose of expediting the transition into doctoral studies.

Michigan State University: Better evidence of predictors for student success–and more nuanced discussions of how we define success–are needed, particularly as institutions respond to changing political climates for discussions about diversity… In 2004 the Graduate School evaluated completion rates for the major university fellowship recipients from 1999-2000… Selection criteria for the programs were changed in 2005 to emphasize "fit" to programs and faculty research areas, leadership and research experience. We will track the completion rates of students selected under the new criteria to see if that change produces better outcomes, and in particular, better success for women and students of color.

University of Georgia: In September and October, two seminars were conducted for faculty… The first seminar focused on designing program websites to attract the best doctoral students (Condition One)… The second seminar focused on how different programs used innovative ways to improve the doctoral admissions process beyond standardized test scores (Condition Two). Four presenters from four departments spoke to approximately 20 participants on strategies and criteria that they have used in their admissions process to increase the likelihood that the students who are admitted will successfully complete their degrees: English: Student writing samples; Adult education: Holistic approach to understanding GRE scores with underrepresented students; Psychology: Fit between program interests and research experiences; Biochemistry/molecular biology: Student interviews/campus visits.

University of Missouri–Columbia: Departments create a post-admissions grid that describes every newly admitted doctoral student according to a set of criteria pertinent to graduate school persistence that includes four common elements across all programs and up to two program-specific predictors. The common elements are: 1) previous undergraduate or graduate research experience; 2) completion of an advanced undergraduate (or beginning graduate) course in research methods, statistics, or theory with a B+ or better; 3) whether the student visited MU prior to making a decision to enroll; and 4) whether the student was offered a position as TA, RA, or a fellowship that qualifies for a fee waiver. Departments choose two additional qualifications that they believe are especially predictive of success in their programs… This initiative was revised to include an additional common element (whether the student was offered a position as a TA, RA, or a fellowship) to provide data on an additional common element, the provision of institutional financial support.

CHAPTER 5
Promising Practices: Mentoring and Advising

Success in achieving a Ph.D. depends upon a close and effective working relationship with one's advisor and mentor. And yet, while virtually every doctoral student has a research advisor, survey data from the Ph.D. Completion Project and other studies show that not every student has access in their doctoral program to someone they consider a mentor (Council of Graduate Schools, 2004; 2009).

Though mentoring is often cited as among the most influential factors on degree completion, that influence is difficult to assess. Student differences in cultural background and field, or discipline, may result in differing perceptions of effective mentoring. For some students, the mentoring that is valued most may be guidance on dissertation research or working with them on publications and presentations; for others, it may be advice about how to navigate a career path after completing the degree; and for others, it may mean providing support and counsel when students are experiencing tough times, including such common obstacles as writer's block, complications in the relationship with one's research advisor or committee, or discouraging experiences on an academic job market.

Mentoring is also an area that can pose unique challenges to universities seeking to implement program-level or university-wide improvements. For example, while research supervision is a formal responsibility of graduate faculty, and is recognized as such within the administrative structure and tenure and promotion processes for faculty career advancement, often universities do not have similar formal structures to require and encourage "mentoring," which is sometimes thought of as going above and beyond the call of research supervision duties (King, 2003). Indeed, some faculty may cling to notions that the qualities of good mentoring are either inborn character traits or else habits that are best acquired and instilled informally (e.g. by example) rather than through professional development.

Because mentoring is practiced and valued unevenly in doctoral programs, and because student expectations of mentors differ, it is not surprising that students report having unequal access to quality mentors as they pursue their Ph.D.s. Some students describe their having access to good mentors in terms of "good luck" (Walker et al., 2008), by contrast to access to their research advisors which is an expectation and understood to be required for degree completion. Some students may have an advisor who effectively doubles as a good mentor, while others may find a faculty member aside from their advisor who can provide additional guidance on research, career, and other topics. Students also report receiving valuable mentoring from their peers in the program as well as from persons outside their department.

Because effective mentoring of Ph.D. students takes such different forms, the promising practices that universities have developed as participants in the Ph.D. Completion Project are varied. Nevertheless, there are themes that cut across these activities, including: improvements in the structures of support between research advisors and doctoral candidates; encouraging more collective responsibility within the program for the success of doctoral candidates; increased clarity and transparency about expectations; and enhancing conflict management processes when conflicts arise between students and advisors.

All the institutions that submitted a pre-project assessment reported a large number of policies related to advising and mentoring. All indicated that the 'graduate handbook [was] available to all new students,' that they provided 'workshops or seminars about teaching techniques or pedagogy,' and that they offered 'professional development workshops or seminars.' Most also reported that a 'program or university ombudsman [was] available to graduate students.' Very few reported that 'Ph.D. completion data [was] used by [the] university in promotion and tenure decisions,' or that they provided 'hint or tip sheets for students about program completion.' Over half of the policies had been in existence for ten or more years; among the more recent innovations, a 'web-based system for tracking student degree progress/milestones' was the most-frequently mentioned.

However, improvements in mentoring and advising outnumber improvements in any other area of activity and innovation in the Ph.D. Completion Project. Overall, the activities below represent the recognition of participating universities that improvements in the quality, frequency, and uniformity of interaction between students and program faculty are among the most promising steps that programs and universities can undertake to increase Ph.D. completion.

Promising Practices

Promising practices identified by participating universities in the area of mentoring and advising include:

Resources for students

- Provide a comprehensive orientation to prepare students for graduate school

- o Initiate comprehensive orientation program
  - o Review and revise current department/program new student orientation activities to promote collaboration with the Office of Graduate Studies and continue orientation activities throughout the first year
  - o Design and pilot test a three-to-five day summer program aimed at preparing incoming underrepresented doctoral students for graduate study and their programs
  - o Hold Graduate Student Information Fair
  - o Continue workshop series to define requirements and reinforce information critical to degree outcomes
  - o Review and revamp orientation programs based on feedback from evaluations and exit interviews
- Develop/revise graduate student handbooks
  - o for the university that address academic, social, and orientation needs
  - o for each program that convey information that is program-specific
  - o for various stages of the Ph.D. process, e.g. first-year doctoral student handbook
- Make expectations and requirements transparent
  - o Develop and review the content of departmental web sites
  - o Clearly articulate program expectations/academic milestones, requiring completion of all pre-dissertation milestones before year four
- Develop/enhance online mechanisms so students and faculty can track progress and offer feedback or communicate with one another
  - o Online milestone tracking systems, "dissertation checklists," electronic portfolios, and annual progress report systems that integrate graduate school records, student input, and evaluative comments from faculty. Such online mechanisms create a framework for greater communication between the graduate school, faculty, and students on student progress in meeting the goals set each year and clarification of goals for the following year. These online resources may also enhance identification of potentially critical times when intervention or communication is needed. Such systems have been tailored to include coursework, annual reviews, teaching materials, thesis proposals, research products, contact information for prospective employers, and file sharing and chat rooms that promote communication with peers and advisors.

Regularity and uniformity of progress review

- Implement regular advisor/advisee meetings and progress reports
- Encourage programs to set up annual student performance review systems
- Develop "best practices" for tracking student progress in relation to the amount and type of student financial aid
- Institute a modified report on students' plans for the remainder of the academic year to be completed immediately upon their advancement to candidacy

Early advising

- Require each first-year student to have an advisor or advisory structure; conduct regular evaluations of progress
- Require faculty advisors to be on campus during advisees' first-year as graduate students
- Encourage the participation of graduate students of color and women in targeted programs (for example, the "Bouchet Fellows" program at Yale University)
- Initiate the "Navigating the System" seminar program to address the theme of inclusion and diversity
- Establish administrative structures for the early identification of, and interventions aimed at retaining, "at-risk" students
- Create omsbud position to support first-year students

Resources for faculty

- Offer workshops for faculty on mentoring
- Make such workshops part of new faculty orientation
- Develop materials/handbooks and online resources for faculty on mentoring
- Offer mini-grants to help faculty develop initiatives aimed at improving the quality of mentoring
- Create a Graduate Program Directors Council to share best practices, to work collaboratively with the Graduate School, and provide programming to strengthen the skills required for effective and innovative leadership of the University's graduate programs
- Recognize excellence in mentoring through faculty awards

Other mentors

- Train peer mentors and ensure that all new students are assigned a trained peer mentor
- Provide students with external mentors

Selected Highlights

Resources for students

Cornell University: We are developing print materials and programming to help faculty become more effective mentors and to help students develop strong relationships with mentors. One of our first steps has been a brief publication for students, which was distributed to new graduate students in Fall 2008. The Graduate School also incorporated a mentoring panel into graduate student orientation programs since Fall 2007. The program, "Establishing and Maintaining Successful Faculty/Student Mentoring Relationships," consists of a panel of students and their faculty mentors who discuss their experience with mentoring relationships. The sessions have been well attended by faculty and graduate students, and the response has been positive.

Marquette University: Selecting a Dissertation Advisor and Configuring a Committee: This workshop for doctoral students will impart strategies for the following: selecting an appropriate dissertation advisor and configuring the dissertation committee; enhancing students' opportunities or productive and successful outcomes in their working relationships with advisors and committee members; engaging more fully in the dissertation process; and becoming more proactive members of the dissertation team.

North Carolina State University: Graduate students at NCSU, as well as students who participated in any of the OPT-ED partner programs, will be invited to attend a special annual symposium for graduate students. Invited experts will address such topics as roles and responsibilities of the mentor and graduate student, how to select a dissertation committee, how to complete the dissertation, and how to find postdoctoral and faculty positions.

University of North Carolina at Chapel Hill: Mentoring tips for students: [T]his topic will be included in the orientation meetings that the Graduate School holds for new graduate students each August… A leading faculty member with a successful mentoring record (perhaps the recipient of the previous year's mentor award) will engage students in a discussion about mentoring and what they can do to facilitate strong, supportive relationships with their faculty advisors. In particular, this discussion session will cover strategies for 1) identifying a research mentor, 2) networking with multiple faculty as 'mentors' during the graduate school tenure, 3) networking with peers as 'peer-mentors' during the graduate school tenure, and 4) how to trouble shoot difficult situations should they arise.

Student Receptions focusing on mentoring: All first and second year students from the participating departments were invited to an informal catered reception that included a panel of advanced students who had agreed to share their experiences as doctoral students and provide advice on successful strategies for moving through their programs.

Regularity and uniformity of progress review

Ohio State University: The [History] department has regularized and rationalized the faculty advisor-student advisee relationship. In 2006-07, the program instituted an itemized set of guidelines for advisors, which are now included in the department's graduate handbook. Faculty members are required to prepare a Course Performance Report on each student in each graduate-level course. These reports evaluate the student's work (with special attention to suggestions for improvement) and include the student's grade for the course. Faculty advisors are expected to maintain regular contact with their advisees for the year and schedule specific "landmark" conferences. Early in the third quarter of study, advisors are required to meet with advisees to discuss progress and plans for the coming year... [In addition, the department instituted a] report form for the two crucial advising sessions. The report, written by the advisor and signed by both advisor and advisee, would summarize the students' progress and outline plans for future study. Delays in completion of program requirements would have to be justified.

University of Missouri–Columbia: MU Graduate School policy requires that all graduate students receive an annual review... [I]n order to ensure that doctoral students in participating programs receive timely and useful feedback, programs participating in the proposed project will make use of a newly developed online progress reporting tool. The on-line report will require students to document completion of required courses and examinations, awards received, and professional accomplishments such as conference presentations and publications. It will also require the student to evaluate his or her own strengths and weaknesses. In response to this self-assessment, the advisor, in turn, will provide a written evaluation of the student's progress towards the degree and the quality of course, research, and teaching or research assistant performance. This online review will serve as the foundation for a face-to-face meeting between the advisor, the student, and his or her committee members to discuss career aspirations and next steps for reaching them. It may also serve as a mechanism to evaluate the fit between the advisor and the student and provide the mechanisms for a discussion about whether or not changing advisors would be desirable.

Early advising

Ohio State University: Faculty advisors must be on campus during the first year of their advisees' graduate program; create omsbud position to support first-year students (Neuroscience).

Yale University: "Navigating the System" Seminar Program: As a component of the Bouchet Fellows Program, the Graduate School, through the Office for Diversity and Equal Opportunity (ODEO), will develop a seminar series that will address the theme of inclusion and diversity in graduate education, particularly with respect to assessing the needs and providing the resources for the professional career development of URMs and women within the academy. Each seminar will include a diverse panel of Graduate School faculty and advanced graduate students from the humanities, social sciences, and sciences… The goal of the "Navigating the System Seminars" is to provide a forum for graduate students to identify specific concerns and discuss how these concerns can be addressed through innovative and thoughtfully developed policies and practices at the Graduate School and departmental levels. These highly participatory discussions will be held every two months (September, November, January, March) during the academic yeResources for faculty

Brown University: Four workshops were developed and planned for directors of graduate study and chairs of departments. These workshops are intended to be environments for exchange of information about available resources, strategies, and practices that may be adapted to departmental situations. The four workshops are:

- Recruiting: strategies for attracting the best applicants and improving yield and diversity within programs
- Transition: mentoring and advising students in their early years
- Research and the Ph.D. Candidate: helping students to plan to accomplish their dissertation research
- Dissertation Completion and Beyond: strategies for completing the dissertation and charting the next steps in academic careers

Based on the active engagement of the faculty who attend, we intend to identify those who are best suited to become the Ph.D. completion project advisors to assist students across the graduate school.

Florida State University: The Office of Graduate Studies will also develop and offer a graduate student supervision workshop for new faculty each fall semester. The foci of these workshops will be to provide valuable information regarding university graduate policies, standards of responsible conduct of research, the role of the Institutional Review Board, copyright/patent information, the importance of annual student assessments, effective techniques for supervising doctoral students, and graduate-education resources available to students (e.g., Workshop Series, RCRC course). Completion rates are increased when it is viewed as a collective responsibility (CGS, 2004). We will coordinate these efforts with the academic deans and the Dean of the Faculties.

Two FSU faculty members awarded $10,000 by OGS and Office of Research to develop [three] mentor/mentee scenarios for the faculty training workshop– will be used to generate interactions between participants and performers. Evaluations will be used to improve these; video tape revised scenarios for future use… There will be two audiences for this activity: the Program of Instructional Excellence (PIE) and the directors of graduate programs. FSU is working on focusing the project and making it have long-term impact… The vignettes will focus on the mentor/mentee relationship and on empowering the mentee. The vignettes will feature the same scene played out with variations three times. The first is a gripe session, the second pulls out salient issues in a realistic scene, and the third offers solutions.

Purdue University: "Mentoring" is the most frequent concern expressed by Ph.D. students. (1) The Graduate School recently changed its graduate faculty appointment policy to require "evidence of successful graduate student mentoring" prior to appointment. New faculty with prior mentoring experience are encouraged to attend mentoring workshops conducted by the Graduate School and faculty without prior mentoring experience are required to attend. (2) Beginning in 2006, the Graduate School hosts a formal reception, attended by faculty, students, and administrators, at which an outstanding graduate student mentor is named. (3) The Graduate School is leading a University-wide program on the responsible conduct of research (RCR) which includes a component on mentoring. Both faculty and graduate students will be required to complete an educational/training program. (4) The University is developing a formal process for review of graduate programs that includes an evaluation of student mentoring. All of these efforts are focused, in whole or in part, with the completion of Ph.D. students.

University of California, Los Angeles: UCLA currently publishes several handbooks outlining faculty and students' rights and responsibilities. We propose to revise both Standards and Procedures, our handbook concerning general policies for graduate study at UCLA, and our Faculty Handbook, which is a faculty advisor's guide. We would like to develop a checklist for each handbook reflecting best practices in graduate education that would allow the user to assess their own level of understanding, as well as to assess whether these practices are in place in their programs… We propose to provide training workshops to new faculty regarding developing productive advisor student relations. We would offer this workshop at the beginning of each academic year. These workshops will utilize the faculty handbook along with presentations from exemplar faculty to develop a common understanding of what fosters useful and productive student/faculty academic relationships.

University of California, San Diego: Develop department workshops and other information-disseminating opportunities for faculty about positive mentoring, and the differences between mentoring and advising. Departments will also consider approaches for faculty development of techniques and approaches for positive student interaction, and team building. Faculty will be encouraged to attend mentoring meetings at professional conferences and bring back information for department distribution.

Other mentors

External mentors

Florida State University: MentorNet is an award-winning national program that uses the internet to link mentors and mentees. MentorNet focuses on the STEM disciplines and links students with mentors in a variety of sectors (e.g. industry, government, non-profits, and academia)… FSU joined MentorNet (e-mentoring) in June 2008. This program provides an 8-month mentoring relationship in addition to the student's on campus mentor. A survey of MentorNet participants revealed that most appreciated the one-on-one mentoring program and that they liked the training and the coaching. Students also liked the e-forum, a web-based discussion group on topics such as work/life balance, as well as the resources for and about mentoring, diversity, careers, etc.

University of Maryland, Baltimore County: The Meyerhoff Graduate Program has a full-time staff member who meets regularly with the fellows in that program… The meetings are weekly for first year students and taper off to monthly for more advanced students. The mentoring can be "intrusive" at times when it is clear that intervention is needed. Meyerhoff fellows also meet regularly with each other to discuss progress in coursework and research as well as non-academic issues. The NSF Bridge to the Doctorate (BD) fellows also receive a similar experience through the PROMISE program.

Peer mentors

Pennsylvania State University: All programs will participate in a peer-to-peer mentoring program for new students, especially women and underrepresented students. Programs will be encouraged to incorporate the McNair Scholars, SROP, and WISE graduates currently in Penn State graduate programs, in addition to their own student bodies. Incorporating graduate students with experience in these programs will reaffirm the importance of the pipelines with institutions that feed to these programs, plus the students themselves can better identify with the new recruits because of their own personal background.

Purdue University: The Graduate School's peer mentoring program offers first-year doctoral students the opportunity to have senior students in their program act as student mentors. Senior students have experience as first-years, developed research areas, have relationships with faculty, and have knowledge of the town and the social environment. Mentors share their experiences and advice for adjusting to graduate school and the new environment to their mentees while answering questions and offering mentees a place to be heard… The objectives for this program include: 1) providing peer support to first-year doctoral students from senior graduate students, 2) facilitating first-year doctoral students' acclimation to graduate school, 3) providing guidance and advice to first-year doctoral students, and 4) helping first-year doctoral students determine if their program is an appropriate fit.

University of Missouri–Columbia: [Graduate] Colleague Circles [consist] of two [or three] advanced doctoral students and a group of 10-15 students in the same or closely related disciplinary or interdisciplinary area. Circle mentors, chosen because of their strong interpersonal skills and success in both research and teaching, will facilitate monthly discussions on topics chosen by the group. Sample topics might include time management, handling professional [and] ethical dilemmas, teaching techniques, [and] negotiating race, ethnic, and gender differences or divides. During each year of the…project, all students newly admitted to doctoral study in participating programs will be encouraged to participate in peer mentoring… Students value peer mentoring experiences and need to have opportunities to ask questions and interact with others who are having similar experiences in graduate school.

Yale University: Since its inception in September 2005, the Bouchet Fellows Program has continued to provide resources to support the particular needs of URMs and women graduate students in the nine participating programs through mentoring activities, seminars, and workshops aimed at addressing graduate student concerns… [The program is seen] as a three-pronged initiative focused on peer-to-peer advising, research career development seminars, and developing "skills as scholars" workshops. This paradigm has proved both valuable and sustainable. In the peer-to-peer advising program, mentors will continue to meet one-on-one with mentees on a monthly basis, and there are also monthly activities provided by the mentoring program, which allow mentors and mentees to get together, usually in a dinner/discussion format.

CHAPTER 6
Promising Practices: Financial Support

Students and researchers often cite financial support as being among the most influential factors on Ph.D. completion and attrition (Bowen and Rudenstine 1992; Nelson and Lovitts 2001; Nettles and Millett, 2006, among others). On the surface, there would appear to be a direct correlation between the financial support package that students receive and the likelihood that they will complete. Fields in which funding for students is relatively plentiful (such as the life sciences) tend to exhibit higher than average completion rates and shorter than average time to degree, whereas in fields where full and continuous funding for students may be less common (such as the humanities), completion rates are typically lower and time to degree, longer.

Below the surface, however, it may be that while some level of funding provides the minimum conditions for a student's degree completion, the structure of financial support and the ways that other factors interact with that support play an equal or even larger role in the likelihood that students will complete. For example, some programs offer continuous funding to students through the summer, while other programs do not; and some universities may have more flexibility than others in the timing and number of teaching and research assistantships allocated to students depending on institutional constraints such as budget, student demand, and university requirements. How student support is structured, and whether or not assistantships can be timed to coincide with students' professional growth needs, can influence degree completion as well as time to degree.

One challenge in studying the effect of financial support on degree completion, nationally, is that some universities and programs that are able to offer doctoral fellowships in amounts greater than the national average may also be in a position to provide extensive support and services to students in other areas that are believed to have a positive impact on completion rates. For example, one factor that has perhaps received the greatest attention by researchers is academic and social integration (Lovitts, 2001). Depending upon how financial support through assistantships and fellowships is structured, it can either enhance or inhibit academic and social integration. Tying fellowships to activities that promote academic and social integration of students is one of the common themes across participating universities that have implemented improvements in financial support for doctoral students.

In the financial support and funding structures category, all the responding institutions who completed the pre-project assessment template reported that they provided 'merit-based graduate fellowships/scholarships' and almost all reported that they provided 'merit-based graduate research or teaching assistantships/stipends' and shared 'information about external fellowships for graduate study.' Few provided 'need-based graduate research or teaching assistantships/stipends' or limited 'the number of semesters that students can teach.' Most of these policies had been in place for 10 or more years.

Promising Practices

The Ph.D. Completion Project supports sustainable interventions and innovative practices in the provision and structuring of financial support designed to optimize completion and enhance academic and social integration. Promising practices identified by participating universities in the area of financial support and structure include:

Increased student support

- Increase stipend levels to the median of the university's peer group in each broad disciplinary area of the graduate school
- Increase the number of selective university fellowship awards
- Increase the number of summer research awards in the humanities and social sciences
- Provide health insurance premium coverage
- Initiate fellowship block grants and supplemental graduate fellowships
- Explore higher stipends for students at the dissertation stage
- Create more one-quarter releases from teaching for students at the dissertation stage
- Increase stipend support for summer research
- Change model for graduate assistantship allocation to a "Ph.D. preferred" model, whereby 80% of doctoral students and 20% of master's students will be funded
- Encourage students to apply for external fellowships
- Address potential IRS tax inequities within graduate student population
- Provide conference travel support [See also Curricular and Administrative Processes and Procedures]

Linking departmental allocations and performance indicators of student completion

- Link continuing graduate assistantship positions/fellowship allocations to strategic performance indicators of satisfactory degree progress

Selected Highlights

Increased student support

Brown University: Fostering of a research environment and a culture of competing for external grants. We are concerned not only with budget relief but also with the necessary professional development involved in building a record of supported research for our students. [The] Graduate School, in conjunction with the Office of the Vice President for Research, [has sponsored workshops to] assist students to identify funding sources and to help train students in the grant-writing process… The workshops [focus] on specific private grant awards (e.g., Fulbright-Hayes), and federal fellowship sources (e.g., Ruth Kirschstein awards). These workshops were done in consultation with the Career Services Center of Brown University, and were structured by specific disciplines: 1) Humanities & Social Sciences; and 2) Biosciences and Physical Sciences. In [May], the Dean hosted the first annual reception to honor [the] 117 graduate student winners of external grants and awards.

Michigan State University: Electrical Engineering (in conjunction with the CGS grant, AGEP, and an MSU Provost's initiative grant) has instituted a mentoring program for students preparing for the qualifying exams. The objective of the four-year Incentive Fellowship project is to increase the number of talented U.S. students (especially women and minorities) with financial need who pass the program's qualifying examination each year during the term of the project. One-semester S-STEM Incentive fellowships will be provided each year to 14 academically talented, financially needy engineering graduate students, enabling them to focus on preparing for the exam rather than working "half" time as teaching or research assistants. Their preparation will be facilitated by participating in structured preparation activities provided by each department.

University of California, Los Angeles: [W]e have been working to improve the amount of full-support available across the campus for doctoral students. This summer we have expanded the number of graduate summer research mentorship awards available to our students. These awards enable students to work exclusively on research projects with a mentor's guidance. It is expected that such projects will encourage early publications and professional presentations.

University of Michigan: The centerpiece of the University's MGE/AGEP efforts has been the successful development of a student funding program for under-represented students in STEM fields… The Rackham Engineering Awards (REA) were designed to address these issues, and crafted specifically for the engineering and science model of graduate education… The pilot program called for fellowship support for the first three years followed by teaching or research assistantships for the last two years… [See later discussion in Chapter

8, under "Selected Highlights" about challenges and revisions to the program]. In the new model, REA students receive full first year fellowship support, but must perform research with an advisor in order to obtain summer funding. The subsequent four years of funding are a mixture of fellowship, research and teaching assistantships... Three cohorts of REA students have passed the milestones of terminating studies with a master's degree and taking their Ph.D. qualifying exams. Of these students, 68% are still pursuing their Ph.D... Furthermore, this number of continuing students is slightly *higher* than that for the overall graduate student population.

Linking departmental allocations and performance indicators of student completion

Brown University: The goal of the guaranteed, multi-year support for students is to provide programs with a stable set of resources to design and implement appropriate training experiences for graduate students. In exchange for this flexibility, allocation of resources is dependent upon the successful and meaningful transit of students through the graduate program... [T]he process allocates funds in a structured manner based on information received from departments. And because [the system] does not assume that every student in every program can complete a doctoral degree in five years, it does not unduly 'punish' students in disciplines that typically take more than five years to complete training. Further, [it] rewards both students and departments that have made efforts to assist students in progressing according to departmental milestones by completing technical and professionalizing experiences.

Howard University: In the area of financial support, we propose to make use of graduate student completion and attrition data (but not time-to degree data) in the determination of monetary allocations to departments. The Graduate School's Financial Support Program is currently under review... As part of this process, we will include an incentive structure for all departments participating in the pilot programs. The incentive measure will speak directly to their award allocations pending the annual evaluation of each program's doctoral completion rate targets... In addition to restructuring the policy in Phase II, continuing GA positions will be held to strategic performance indicators of satisfactory degree progress. The key milestone indicators evaluated are time to candidacy and post-candidacy progress. In other words, the amount of continued departmental Graduate Assistantship funding will be based on the degree progress of students recommended for funding.

University of California, Los Angeles: UCLA's QGE [Quality of Graduate Education] program has been used to support innovative departmental practices to improve the quality of graduate education by linking performance indicators to monetary allocation. As a part of our participation in the Completion Project, we have begun to emphasize departmental record of completion as a factor in decisions to allocate funds. Further, departments have been encouraged, using this vehicle, to assess how any requested exceptions, or changes to departmental policy may impact completion and for doctoral students. We have also used completion as an outcome to assess the effectiveness of the QGE program by looking at QGE support and student outcomes among departments with similar departmental characteristics.

University of California, San Diego: Commit the Dean of Graduate Studies to increase the amount of fellowship funding that is available to graduate students by one million dollars per year, and to connect funding allocations with department completion/continuation improvement efforts and data. OGS and departments will promote external fellowships with staff help for proposal development and submission. Special efforts will be directed to acquisition of NIH and NSF supplements targeting underrepresented students and women.

CHAPTER 7
Promising Practices: Program Environment

The academic "environment" of a Ph.D. program is shaped by department-led and university-wide efforts to create the conditions for high expectations, high performance, and strong student support. The majority of students' interactions with faculty and peers in a doctoral program take place in the formal spaces of the classroom, the laboratory, or the advisor's office. But much of the social interaction that may be conducive both to degree completion and to the adoption of a professional identity in the discipline occurs outside of these formal research spaces. A comfortable graduate student lounge, for example, with professional publications, bulletin boards listing activities in the discipline, and visible recognition of student achievements can provide a space for students to exchange information and to begin the process of assimilating into the social circle of their chosen discipline (Nelson and Lovitts, 2001). Campus-wide organizations and graduate student centers can provide professional development and networking opportunities, and can foster interdisciplinary discussion and community building. Informal opportunities to participate in department events, regular social gatherings, or team sports may also prove to be important components of a graduate student's socialization to their academic discipline.

All the institutions that submitted a pre-project assessment reported that 'graduate students [are] invited to serve on university committees,' that they have a 'university graduate student organization/group' and that 'guest speakers [are] invited from outside the program or university.' A majority reported that 'faculty/student discussions about graduate programs [are] encouraged.' Most of these policies and practices had been in place for 10 years or more although a few institutions reported that they had implemented some of these practices more recently.

Promising Practices

The Ph.D. Completion Project supports interventions and innovative practices designed to enhance both the formal as well as the informal spaces that comprise the environment of Ph.D. programs. Promising practices identified by participating universities in the area of enhancing the program and university environment include:

Support networks and support services

- Initiate campus-wide efforts to bring students together across disciplines and within the department for academic and social interaction
- Encourage graduate student organizations in all programs/departments to explore community building activities
- Promote involvement of graduate students as members of campus-wide or department-wide committees to promote their career development, campus networking, and connection to the campus
- Promote faculty and staff participation in conferences and workshops focused on graduate student services, retention, and development
- Highlight achievements and accomplishments of graduate students through newsletters, dinners, or other venues
- Develop a network for support
- Doctoral Student Connection – A facilitated blogging system that enables communication and forms a network between doctoral students
- Monthly support group for minority students
- Affinity groups or professional associations
- Update institution and program webpages to provide an overview of initiatives to improve Ph.D. completion and highlight efforts to create a more nurturing environment where students can be successful
- Outreach to and integration of fellows
- Offer retention support and intervention services
- Offer conflict resolution workshops
- Establish a Graduate Student Commons as a center for graduate student activities, both academic and social, to promote greater interaction among students of all disciplines.

Family accommodation policies

- Implement a Parental Accommodation Policy
- Develop institution-wide policy on family and medical leave for graduate assistants

Selected Highlights

Support networks and support services

Marquette University: The number of underrepresented minority students in Marquette's doctoral program is smaller then we would like (8%). This often results in students feeling isolated. A support group that encompasses all programs will be established and conduct monthly meetings that address topics of their choosing. Social activities will follow each session. The group will be coordinated by the Associate Provost for Diversity, with guidance from the Director of the Counseling Center. Advisors will actively encourage students to participate.

North Carolina State University: The Graduate School will embark [on] a new Capital Campaign effort to raise funds for a Graduate Student Commons which will be a center for graduate student activities, both academic and social, to promote greater interaction among students of all disciplines.

Purdue University: This specific intervention would enhance the current programming for fellows, including development of a "fellow ambassadors" program and recognition of academic milestones achieved. Enhancements to the Fellows Community, a web-based resource utilizing the university course-management system including links and resources specific to fellows, such as medical insurance and vision in addition to creating a dialogue on academic and social integration, would be integrated. Development is underway with some activities implemented such as the web-based resource and workshops on taxes and insurance for fellows.

University of California, Los Angeles: Each quarter the Graduate Division publishes the Graduate Quarterly, which is a newsmagazine geared towards highlighting the achievements of graduate students and providing information which may be of interest to master's and doctoral students.

University of Georgia: With regard to promoting communication among those involved in doctoral education, a Problem Solving Forum was created. This forum contains difficult situations encountered by doctoral students and encourages doctoral students and faculty to offer their suggestions… [S]ubmissions to the Problem Solving Forum are frequent and several doctoral students have reported this feature has been of utility to them.

University of Illinois–Urbana Champaign: The Graduate College continues to meet with its Graduate Student Advisory Group in order to discuss what services and interventions they believe are most needed for their completion and success. Graduate students meet with Graduate College deans twice per semester to discuss these important issues… In 2007-2008, the Graduate College offered over 40 workshops for graduate students. Topics addressed a full scope of issues from acclimation and skills for success in graduate school to completion and career transition… To communicate directly with over 10,000 graduate students enrolled at Illinois, the Graduate College publishes *GradLinks*. In 2008 we began distributing *GradLinks* as a weekly e-mail bulletin to provide students with brief updates about important deadlines, administrative procedures, campus policy, events, and opportunities. *GradLinks* enables direct communication with graduate students across campus.

[W]e began the Ph.D. Completion Project Speakers Series during the Spring of 2007… This program will run twice a year and targets a wide audience of graduate students as a means to build community and break down the isolation of graduate study. Our inaugural speaker, Jorge Cham, attracted an audience of over 200 students, creating a standing-room-only environment. Students stayed long after the speaker concluded his witty, but insightful, commentary on the Ph.D. completion process. They met the author, had books signed, and stayed on for a social hour.

University of North Carolina at Chapel Hill: Mentoring, with a focus on "at risk" groups: The Graduate School also hosted a "Women in Science" Dinner for doctoral students in those science departments participating in the Ph.D. Completion Project. The event focused on peer networking within departments. The Dean spoke briefly before the dinner and encouraged the students to brainstorm strategies for building peer networks that would lead to successful degree completion. Feedback indicated that this was a good venue for the women to network and problem-solve and several felt inspired to go back to their departments and organize more of these types of meetings. Finally, the Graduate School sponsored a lecture by…a nationally recognized research chemist and an outspoken critic of the culture of academic science… Over 100 students and faculty attended [the] lecture and the more informal one-on-one sessions that followed the lecture.

Family accommodation policies

Duke University: [O]ur Office of Graduate Student Affairs worked with graduate student groups and other units to craft and implement a new Childbirth & Adoption Accommodation Policy… this policy will allow caregivers of newborns or newly adopted children to care for them full time in the first weeks after the birth or adoption… We believe this new policy will make Duke more competitive with its peer institutions and will promote a healthy work-life balance for its students.

Cornell University: We have implemented a new Graduate Student Parental Accommodation Policy which provides [six] weeks paid leave to funded student parents upon the birth or adoption of a child or acute child illness. We initiated university-level discussions about the need for child care that have resulted in the construction of a new campus child care facility that opened in Fall 2008. We have also strengthened our Child Care Grants program for student parents.

In partnership with Cornell health professionals, we have refined a case management approach for students in distress that allows us to provide services at the field level.

Howard University: A second intervention producing progress in our retention efforts is a *Leave of Absence for Exceptional Family Circumstances* policy added to the Graduate School's *Rules and Regulations for the Pursuit of Academic Degrees.* The new policy recognizes the circumstances surrounding childbirth, adoption, illness, disability, caring for incapacitated dependents, and military service. The requested amount of time may vary due to the circumstances and formal feedback from the student's faculty advisor. Students returning from approved leave of absence are not required to apply for readmission to the Graduate School.

Pennsylvania State University: In January 2008 the university introduced the "New Parent Accommodation" guideline…[which] enables assistants who shoulder parental care responsibilities for new children to be relieved of their primary assistantship duties and academic obligations up to six weeks. Graduate assistants retain their salary and all university benefits and privileges during the accommodation period.

University of Maryland, Baltimore County: [T]he Graduate School and the GSA collaborated to create a new draft of the Graduate Assistant leave policy guidelines document that includes paid vacation, sick leave, and maternity leave policies. These new policy guidelines have since been approved and implemented as of March 2008.

CHAPTER 8
Promising Practices: Research Experience

Scholars in different disciplines conduct research and publish results in very different ways. In the lab sciences, students spend large portions of time as members of a research team, whereas in the humanities students typically pursue their research individually. In the former setting, joint publication is common, whereas in the latter collaborative authorship remains the exception rather than the norm. Generally, it is in their doctoral programs that students first experience the full extent of these differences. These differences and their implications for a student's definition of and progress on the dissertation may affect completion rates and time to degree.

Another influential field difference is the extent to which dissertation stage research is a continuation of, or marks a major break with, coursework. In some fields, students have little or no preparation for the dissertation-level research required once they finish coursework and complete their qualifying or comprehensive examinations. Students may, therefore, spend years in a program before gaining a full understanding of what a doctorate in the discipline will entail. In such instances, students may feel they lack the early support and guidance they need to complete with confidence.

Such field differences imply different models of the individual's contribution to a doctoral degree as well as different social contexts for that contribution. Researchers often note that the degree of social interaction characteristic of the sciences, where an apprenticeship model, research teams, and a laboratory setting prevail, can provide a more supportive environment than the solitary, individual research with often extended periods without advisor feedback that is often characteristic of the humanities (Council of Graduate Schools, 2004; Nerad & Cerny, 1991; de Valero, 2001; Nettles & Millett, 2006).

Promising Practices

The Ph.D. Completion Project supports interventions and innovative practices in addressing differences in the research experience that may affect doctoral degree completion and attrition. The interventions include: (1) pre-program research experiences (prior to starting the doctoral program) that help prepare students–particularly underrepresented students–for doctoral study; and (2) early research experiences including several lab rotations for science students and summer research experiences for humanities and social sciences students who may not otherwise be exposed to research until much later in the career.

A third category–exposure to professional development opportunities through seminars, conferences, etc.–is discussed in Chapter 9. Some promising practices include:

Pre-program research experiences

- Identify top undergraduates and invite them to participate in a research institute late in their sophomore year to prepare and recruit these students to pursue doctoral studies [See also 'Selection and Admissions']
- Enhance an intensive 8-week summer research institute experience for recipients of the university Merit Fellow Awards (underrepresented students) [See also 'Selection and Admissions']
- Offer summer Pre-Doctoral Institute for underrepresented students/ "Early Start Program"

Early research experiences

- Encourage lab rotations prior to choosing a mentor/research area
- Provide opportunities and funding for humanities and social sciences students to participate in structured research in the early stages of their programs and to attend professional meetings
- Provide students with a catalog of research opportunities and facilitate matching of research interests between advisors and students
- Streamline course requirements to allow students the opportunity to engage early in research

Selected Highlights

Pre-program research experiences

Cornell University: Design and pilot test a three-to-five day summer program aimed at preparing incoming underrepresented doctoral students (selected by nomination/invitation) for graduate study and their programs. The goals of this activity include better preparation for students' participation in the academic enterprise as a scholar, full integration of URM students into the fields, and, ultimately, successful student performance and degree completion.

University of Michigan: The Summer Institute is an intensive 8 week experience for recipients of the Rackham Merit Fellow Awards (underrepresented students). The program takes place in the summer prior to the students' first year in graduate school. In Year 2004-2005 a research component was added to the Summer Institute for those students in engineering and the sciences. The purpose of this change was to provide students with early research experiences, either through laboratory rotations or involvement in one particular research project… The program objectives are to strengthen and increase the success rate of Rackham Merit Fellowship (RMF) students, provide an academically challenging introduction to graduate studies, connect incoming students with faculty mentors and research opportunities. It also provides a social and professional transition to graduate student life. This year, 2008, participants came from a variety of fields. In particular, students from Anthropology, English and Women's Studies, Mechanical Engineering, Molecular, Cellular and Developmental Biology as well as Nuclear Engineering and Radiological Science participated in the Institute… Evaluations are assessed each summer. We have many testimonials from participating and former students and have conducted several focus groups. Thus far our feedback has been exceptionally positive, with some few exceptions, from both students and faculty. We are studying and comparing the progress made by students who participate in the Summer Institute program both before and after the early research intervention was implemented.

Early research experiences

Howard University: The Office of Retention, Mentoring, and Student Support Programs will annually catalog research projects being conducted by members of the graduate faculty at Howard. This data source will include the PI's name, title of the project, abstract, current staffing and Graduate Assistant (GA) requests. In addition, we will contact each doctoral student in the pilot departments to track whether they currently have a research appointment. If not, we will match the student with a research project closely aligned to their specialization and facilitate the student joining the research team.

Michigan State University: Plant Biology is tracking the outcomes of students who enter the program in a specific lab and the outcomes of those who choose an advisor after several lab rotations. Nearly half of entering Plant Biology students do optional rotations in up to three laboratories during their first two semesters in the program; the other half enter directly into the lab of a faculty member whom they have identified as their advisor. The department wants to look at the effects these modes of entering the program have on completion outcomes, specifically around questions of integration into the department, time spent in choosing a research topic, and time-to-degree.

Ohio State University: Chemistry has also started to work on the financial packages available to its students and has worked creatively with its endowment funds to create additional offers to 8-10 of its 45 incoming students. These small awards, which are on top of the regular awards, are meant to help move new graduate students into the lab environment faster, which Chemistry anticipates will help enhance the student's experience and lead to less attrition and faster completion.

Pennsylvania State University: All programs will implement means by which to engage doctoral students in research at earlier points in their graduate careers… [For example, Physics proposed to] [s]treamline course requirements to enable students to focus on research earlier in their careers and to [s]ponsor opportunities for women and underrepresented students participating in NSF-funded summer programs associated with the Material Research Center at the Pennsylvania State University to meet program faculty and graduate students

University of Cincinnati: The College of Medicine has developed an innovative approach …with the Biomedical Sciences Flex Program… Students complete a core curriculum in cell and molecular biology, research ethics, and several elective courses in [the first year] along with laboratory rotations that cross traditional departmental lines. Students who successfully complete the first year then choose a graduate program to enter and complete the curriculum and requirements of that program… The Flex program provides an interesting opportunity to evaluate the effects of several variables on Ph.D. completion. Some aspects of the program seem likely to increase the prospects for degree completion, e.g., the early professional experience afforded by laboratory rotations and the ability of the students to delay their choice of program entry until they have more information. Other aspects, however, may work against completion since these students have an indeterminate status in the critical first year of graduate study.

University of North Carolina at Chapel Hill: One way to foster [the identification of students as researchers and scholars] is to involve students in the activities of their own professional organizations and to encourage them to present their research findings at those meetings… Moreover, it is important for students to remain actively involved in scholarly or research activities throughout the year, including the summer months. Whereas students in the sciences usually find resources to support their research during the summer (within their mentors' laboratory or in the laboratory of other faculty members), this is much more difficult for students in the humanities/social sciences. Therefore, we propose to create a fund that will provide support for travel to professional meetings (for students in both the sciences/engineering as well as the humanities/social sciences). In addition, this fund will also provide resources for other research costs such as access to data bases, materials for data collection and/or attendance at focused summer workshops for skill training (targeted for students in the humanities/social sciences).

CHAPTER 9
Promising Practices: Curricular and Administrative Processes and Procedures

Although this chapter is titled "Curricular and Administrative Processes and Procedures," the following discussion encompasses other broader aspects of programmatic structure and environment that at first glance seem to be outside this area. For example, we group initiatives aimed at providing support for writing during the dissertation stage (or earlier stages) or offering various types of professional development opportunities under this heading. These types of workshops and supports are critical elements of program quality—as such, they belong under curricular and administrative processes and procedures (and arguably, under Program Environment as well).

One of the most far-reaching activities supported by the Ph.D. Completion Project is the adoption by participating institutions of new university-wide systems, or the enhancement of existing systems, for collecting and using data. Many universities are, for the first time, systematically tracking attrition and using completion and attrition data to assess and review doctoral programs. In order to use these data more effectively, they are revising quantitative data collection methods; implementing exit surveys for completing and departing students; tracking student departures from doctoral study; and analyzing patterns of attrition for their potential relation to other factors (such as financial support and university policies). Participating universities are also incorporating data on completion and attrition into the regular program review process, and using data to institutionalize best practices in other areas of intervention (e.g. selection and admissions, professional development) across all programs through campus-wide initiatives. In addition, universities are streamlining their administrative processes to make them more transparent and user-friendly and departments are examining sequencing of courses and other requirements to ensure they offer smooth transitions.

Another major initiative being undertaken by the participating institutions is to provide writing assistance to all doctoral students, in particular those at the dissertation stage. There is widespread recognition that students at the dissertation stage feel isolated and vulnerable and universities are putting into place a number of efforts to help students overcome these feelings and remain on track. These often involve bringing students together for some kind of a retreat or "boot camp," providing intensive writing assistance, and fostering collegiality and camaraderie among them. A second level of effort provides professional development workshops and opportunities to help students understand what is involved in becoming a professional–for example, by providing travel funds so students can attend conferences and present papers and network with others in their field. Some of these workshops are directed towards helping teaching assistants become more effective teachers.

All the institutions that completed the pre-project assessment template reported that 'graduate students outcomes [are] included in program evaluation' and that a 'periodic review of [the] graduate program [is] conducted.' Those responding to the 2007 factor assessment template indicated that they provide 'personal/mental health/issues counseling.' About a third of the policies were newly implemented and a majority of institutions reported establishing at least one new policy, practice or program within the past two years. 'Person/ group delegated responsibility for analysis/reporting of university completion/ attrition data' and 'goals for completion and/or attrition established' were among the most commonly-mentioned new policies.

Promising Practices

Promising practices identified by participating universities include:

Administrative/curricular processes and procedures

- Create/enhance institutional database on students via a web-based system to track student aid types
- Monitor and track all students who leave
  - o Identify students who fail to enroll each quarter/semester
  - o Determine reasons for non-enrollment and plans for future enrollment
  - o Study student data from the past ten years to assess patterns of attrition versus short-term enrollment gaps
  - o Assess the relationship between official leaves of absence, enrollment and attrition
- Introduce a continuous enrollment policy, which will serve as the impetus for students to stay on track and work collaboratively with their mentors towards their final goal of completing the degree
- Expand and refine graduate school and departmental policies and practices for matriculation, and track and report on Ph.D. student degree progress
- Enhance record-keeping and clarifying policy issues at the graduate school, including clarification and creation of policy relevant to doctoral completion and posting of completion figures for programs on website
- Conduct exit surveys of both doctoral recipients and students who do not complete their doctoral work, and use feedback from surveys to develop solutions to reduce attrition

- Revise program review process to examine quality of each graduate program in terms of quality inputs, outcomes, and operational practices; include information and collected data on time-to-degree in review process to ensure department chairs have the necessary data needed to implement appropriate program modifications [See also Financial Support]
- Modify the sequencing of courses and make specific curricular modifications to participating programs
- Create "Direct BS to Ph.D." program

Writing assistance for graduate students

- Offer a writing assistance program for graduate students at all stages through trained writing coaches or writing consultants (senior-level graduate students trained in writing)
- Offer writing courses, workshops, and individual writing consultation with instructors from the Writing Institute (or other similar departments)
- Offer targeted writing services to support international graduate students
- Offer writing assistance to groups of students from several disciplines so they can appreciate the commonality of writing difficulties
- Offer writing groups focused on the comprehensive examinations facilitated by trained ABDs
- Offer a writing clinic geared toward predoctoral students at any level who are working on a manuscript for publication in a peer reviewed journal

Support during the dissertation phase

- Offer a Dissertation Retreat/Dissertation Boot Camp/Dissertation House/ Dissertation Writing Institute for students who are stalled in their progress that offers uninterrupted time to focus on the dissertation, writing strategies, receive feedback, and build peer support
- Provide support through a graduate writing consultant and graduate writing tutors who offer face-to-face tutoring and assistance
- Establish a Doctoral Student Writing Room, where doctoral students could engage in project development, research and writing and collaborate with others
- Offer a Dissertation Writing Residency Fellowship for the 8-week summer period for students (especially from underrepresented groups) not yet making consistent progress at the writing stage of the dissertation
- Offer workshops on time management strategies, especially for students in the final writing stages of their program
- Partner with graduate student organizations to organize dissertation writing workshops with students in broad interdisciplinary groups

- Offer a safe, hospitable space in which graduate students engage in micro-teaching activities, videotape themselves teaching, and engage in the peer review of teaching to develop skills in constructive peer teaching review
- Publicize the PFF program and collaborate with other offices to provide more programming for PFF fellows
- Offer a structured set of professional development workshops to enhance professional skills that are key to a successful doctoral and professional career tailored to whether students are just starting their program, in the middle, or at the dissertation stage
- Offer a University Graduate Certification in College Teaching, designed to help graduate students organize and develop their teaching experience in a systematic and thoughtful way, through workshop experiences in 5 competency areas (adult students as learners and creating learning environments; discipline-related teaching strategies; assessment of learning; technology in the classroom; professional development through an understanding of the academy) and a mentored teaching experience
- Provide travel funds for attending conferences
- Offer a Graduate Teaching Fellowship Program to provide mentored teaching experiences for qualified students who might not normally have such an opportunity in their own discipline, perhaps in conjunction with PFF
- Offer enrichment events aimed at preparing students for job applications and interviews or preparing them for careers in other sectors

Selected Highlights

Administrative/curricular processes and procedures

Florida State University: Four workshops offered during Fall 2008 orientation on selecting/working with major professor and committee; steps to degree; using blackboard; and funding graduate education… Annual workshop for graduate program directors. Topics included results of the Ph.D. Completion Exit Survey; new online graduate program directors' handbook; online tracking system; separate session for new directors. [FSU plans] to host monthly brown bags to improve communication with other university offices.

University of Georgia: Several university-wide policies have been implemented with the overarching goal of improving doctoral completion rates. First, the particular practices that were deemed effective in the original programs from Phase I will be integrated in all doctoral programs at the university. In particular, the doctoral completion data templates, program assessments, research and conferences/meetings will involve all programs. The data for each doctoral program [were] posted in January 2008. Second, the Graduate School is implementing policies that send the message that "all doctoral students are important." Specifically, each student that leaves a program, either through graduation, withdrawal, or transfer, must complete a follow-up survey per new university-wide policy. Additionally, program coordinators will be required to complete a Non-completer Report about each student who leaves their program. Results of these instruments will provide information regarding reasons for completion or noncompletion. Third, a continuous enrollment policy was established to ensure that students' path toward doctoral completion remains as uninterrupted as possible. Last, a publicity awareness campaign is [in] the beginning stage of its implementation. The purpose of this campaign is to communicate the critical issues regarding doctoral noncompletion and promote awareness of this topic.

University of Michigan: The Rackham Graduate School…has developed a web-based navigator that enables students, departments and allied administrative units an opportunity to improve the doctoral education process. The GradTools and Dissertations Checklist system facilitates clear identification of a doctoral program's steps and processes–tailored to the specific requirements of departments–for each student. Through this resource, students, faculty advisors, departments, and the Rackham Graduate School are able to monitor the individual's progress, including when milestones are achieved, requirements yet to be completed, etc. Major features of GradTools include: 1) Dissertation Checklist. Documents the major steps in the process that a student will follow; Schedule. Provides a single place to record events, dates; 2) Resources. This is a site where documents can be shared, stored and organized, and includes links to important resources which assist with the research and writing of the dissertation; 3) Discussion. Permits general discussion on program related matters. Committee members and the students can interact online to comment on dissertation drafts; 4) Help. Provides instructions on how to use GradTools and other technical matters… Strengths of GradTools from student perspectives include the archiving capacity for documents they accumulate during their career in a secure location, the ability to give faculty committee members access to their sites to facilitate immediate review of students' work, as well as ability to use GradTools as a job search tool by creating a resources folder to which potential employers can have review access… This technology has the potential to benefit all of Rackham's graduate programs… We have made it available to all of Rackham doctoral programs. We believe this technology will increase the likelihood of student success, heighten participant satisfaction and contribute to a reduction of time to degree.

Yale University: Launched in spring 2006, the 2-4 Project required every Ph.D. program at Yale to conduct a self-assessment, with particular focus on opportunities for improvement relating to years 2, 3 and 4 of Ph.D. students' careers when coursework is being completed and work on the dissertation begins. Interventions established following the self-assessment vary by department, but include new courses in research methods, curricular changes to better match qualifiers to coursework, changes in the number of courses, improved transitions from courses to research, formalized expectations for participation in field workshops, improved communication between faculty and students, regular evaluations of students, peer mentoring, clear guidance on expectations for the qualifying exam and prospectus, better enforcement of deadlines for the qualifying exam, revised oral exams, standardized schedules for when oral exams are taken, and dissertation colloquia and chapter conferences in some departments. The directors of graduate studies meet regularly with the Deans to discuss issues raised through the 2-4 Project.

Writing assistance for graduate students

Brown University: Through conversation with faculty [and students], we found that writing issues occur not only at the end of graduate training, but throughout. Therefore we revised our plans for a 'dissertation writing institute' into a writing assistance program for graduate students at all stages. In consultation with our writing center…[we hosted a seminar] by…a Senior Lecturer in English, [outlining] concepts and methods essential to translating research into coherent and effective writing. We also hired three writing center coaches–senior level graduate students who received extra training in writing– to provide writing assistance, coaching and editing for graduate students. Since the launch of this project in October 2008, the writing coaches have logged in over 200 hours of writing assistance to graduate students; this is at least 100 hours over the usage of the writing center at comparable times in 2007.

Duke University: The Graduate School supports two services for international graduate students beyond the course offerings of the English for International Student (EIS) program. These are particularly important sources of support for later-year students, as the EIS courses are typically taken in the early years of study. First, at Duke's Writing Studio, international graduate students can work on any writing assignment or project, including proposals, journal articles, and the dissertation, with trained writing tutors. The Studio now has an ESL specialist and all tutors are trained to work specifically with non-native speakers. Second, analogous opportunities for speaking are provided through the EIS program's Oral Skills Coaching service. Students can meet in one-on-one sessions with an experienced ESL speaking coach to develop and rehearse any type of oral presentation.

Marquette University: Writing Consultant Program: Now in its third year… this program has resulted in the training of 14 Graduate Writing Consultants who are Ph.D. students [who] serve within their disciplines to help their peers improve their writing skills across all the writing genres and to make them better prepared for writing the dissertation. Among the experiments being conducted during the grant period [is] the feasibility of training at the same time students from a wide range of disciplines. The professor has managed up to six disciplines in last summer's training session [and] found that, rather than diluting the effort, the diversity helps the trainees appreciate more the commonality of writing difficulties and improves their abilities to be helpful without being judgmental. The training includes critique sessions in which each trainee's writing is discussed by all… Those who have served as Graduate Writing Consultants report that their understanding of the writing process and their own writing have greatly improved, and they feel more comfortable and confident in moving among the various genres of their disciplines. The training makes them less judgmental and more comfortable in relating to others. Happily, those who have received support include first year students who have been helped to see writing as a tool that allows them to deepen their understanding of a subject and to apply that understanding in new ways. Hence, the burden many beginners bear of unrealistic expectations on their writing prowess is being turned into a positive force. Others who have received support include ESL students, and several who were preparing papers for conferences and publication. One of our aims is early intervention, so that improved writing in the beginning year can mature over time and also help improve students' academic performance.

Michigan State University: English, Neuroscience and Sociology are participating in a pilot program to train current ABD's to facilitate writing groups focused on the comprehensive exams. This program is being coordinated by the Graduate School and the Writing Center, which runs both a successful university-wide workshop called "Navigating the Ph.D." (focused in part on comprehensive examination preparation), and small, facilitated dissertation writing groups. The comprehensive exam preparation groups will be a hybrid of these two ongoing projects.

Neuroscience initiated a writing clinic in fall 2008 geared toward predoctoral students at any level who are working on a manuscript for publication in a peer reviewed journal. The workshop participants looked at articles and books on scientific writing, and engaged in discussions of elements of good writing style, the purpose of a paragraph, and tips for achieving clarity in writing. As a group, students edited one or two paragraphs of each student's current writing; they also submitted their writing to other clinic participants. The aims of the writing clinic were to: 1) improve writing skills of the participants; 2) remove psychological barriers that often impede writing; 3) teach students to give and take constructive feedback on their writing; and 4) result in manuscripts submitted for publication. Neuroscience will track how many manuscripts were submitted and accepted.

English implemented a Dissertation Writing Practicum for Ph.D. students in 2008-9 [in the form of monthly workshops]. After the pilot year, they plan to require all post-exam Ph.D. candidates to enroll in the practicum at least once while they are in the program. Students who wish to take the practicum for three credit hours or more would be required to use their participation in the workshops to produce a substantial piece of writing (e.g. a dissertation proposal; a chapter of the dissertation, an article for publication); students taking it for less than three hours would be required to attend and participate in all of the sessions.

Support during the dissertation phase

Marquette University: Our first-ever Dissertation Boot Camp was held June 2-6, 2008, and was a huge success. Eighteen students and four faculty facilitators participated in the Boot Camp. All of the students reported that they made significant progress on their dissertations, and in at least one case a student who had been at a mental roadblock for several years experienced a breakthrough that has allowed her to resume making progress on the dissertation… One of the major suggestions that came from the Dissertation Boot Camp was to establish a dedicated Doctoral Student Writing Room. This would be an area where doctoral students engaged in project development, research and writing could come to work, collaborate with others, and develop a sense of community among these students that can become somewhat isolated. We are working with the university to find such a location.

University of Illinois, Urbana–Champaign: This past year, we launched two important programs targeted at Ph.D. students that work in tandem to address the issues most pressing to completion. The first program – the Dissertation Writing Residency Fellowship (DWR)…is an 8-week writing-intensive summer program aimed at addressing dissertation-writing obstacles. In addition to providing support for students to make progress on their dissertations, the goal of this residency is to assist students in developing life-long writing skills and habits, and large project management abilities that will make them more effective scholars. The Graduate College awarded seven fellowships, each carrying a stipend of $3,000 for the 8-week summer. In addition to the stipend, all typical waivers and fees for this fellowship term were provided. Selected Fellows came from one of four departments (Educational Psychology, English, History, and Political Science)… Fellows are promising students who have been successful at each previous stage of degree progress, but are not yet making consistent progress at the writing stage of the dissertation. Faculty members were especially encouraged to nominate students from underrepresented groups… This experimental program is designed to address what research has shown to be a particularly vulnerable phase in the graduate programs of students pursuing doctorates in the humanities and the interpretive social science–conceptualizing the idea and the plan that will enable them to work effectively toward completing a dissertation. Fellows are present each weekday at the Writers' Workshop on the Urbana campus between the hours of 9:00 am and 3:30 pm during the tenure of their fellowship. They are supported by a Writing Director and Graduate Assistant, and have dedicated workspace, concentrated work time without distraction, and programming relevant to their efforts.

University of Maryland, Baltimore County: The Dissertation House (DH) is designed to facilitate students' progression through the doctoral dissertation process by providing the professional consultation, guidance, and support necessary for scholarly research and writing. The Dissertation House project is based on the successful Scholar's Retreat…at the University of Colorado at Denver… PROMISE: Maryland's Alliance for Graduate Education and the Professoriate, one of the nation's 21 AGEP programs funded by the National Science Foundation, [adapted similar strategies now used by UMBC's Dissertation Coach in] her "TA-DA! Thesis and Dissertation Accomplished - Finally Finished" books and software… In Phase II, we expanded our Dissertation House activities to include a winter session as well as a summer session.

University of Missouri–Columbia: "Writing Saturdays." Once a month we reserve a room in the library and invite a trusted faculty member to present on one aspect of the writing process (with an eye on dissertations). Following the half-hour presentation, a dean joins students in a large reading room in the library to work [for five hours on writing]. Students can also disperse to other areas of the library. Over the course of the first seven months, we've averaged about 25 students showing up, about 15 of whom have become regulars. We design the sessions to be friendly and encouraging–and the deans, themselves, have found the free space for writing to be extremely useful!

Professional development for graduate students

Florida State University: [B]ased on data from exit survey (many grads unaware of workshops), OGS is advertising PFF workshops, including on the FSU campus TV channel… In about 2006, the graduate school took responsibility for FSU's PFF programs and developed new partners in this effort, including the office of research and career services. There is now greater cooperation; for example, the office of research allows PFF fellows to participate in programming for first-year faculty, e.g. about grants... The PFF program has a presence on Blackboard, and students can register for access to the PFF site. PFF programs are open to all doctoral and terminal master's students, as well as postdocs... FSU is tracking participation in professional development programs such as PFF and FSU fellows. In 2006-07, 14 professional development workshops for graduate students were held, with 306 participants. In 2007-08, 14 professional development activities were held, with 426 participants. And in 2008-09, 17 professional development workshops were held, with 806 participants, and two more events scheduled for the academic year. In addition, 3 undergraduate workshops on demystifying graduate school were held. Workshops are typically held at 5:30 p.m. [to enhance attendance].

North Carolina State University: The Preparing the Professoriate (PTP) program is a long-standing program at NC State that gives faculty and doctoral students the opportunity to engage in a mentored teaching activity for an academic year. It is a central component of NC State's attempt to enrich and improve the way in which graduate students are provided with a hands-on teaching opportunity under a distinguished faculty mentor who is recognized for his/her teaching skills. The program is open to doctoral students who plan careers as research/teaching scholars at colleges and universities. The program consists of an observation semester and a teaching or co-teaching semester. In order to participate in the program, students must have completed 18 graduate credit hours in their major prior to the teaching semester, must be in good academic standing in their department, and must be at a point in their doctoral program where they have sufficient time to work with a Faculty Teaching Mentor. The program sponsors 7 workshops for participants throughout the academic year illuminating various aspects of college/university teaching. Currently, 10 doctoral students are selected for the program through a University-wide competition. Each of these students receives a $2,000 stipend and a transcript notation indicating their participation in the program. The aim is to raise the number of participants to at least 20.

Purdue University: The Bilsland Strategic Initiatives Fellowship program provides an opportunity for graduate students, under the direction of a faculty member, to impact graduate education by addressing a graduate school strategic initiative. The fellowship provides an $18,000 stipend for tuition and fees, $1,500 for their project, and a medical insurance supplement. Students write a 3-5 page proposal when applying for the fellowship, and the fellows get experience administering a grant. Sample graduate school strategic initiatives include attracting external and internal sources of funding; enhancing recruitment and retention of graduate students to increase the number, quality, and diversity; emphasizing mentoring relationships between faculty and students; fostering interdisciplinary graduate education; and improving services to enhance the quality of life for graduate students.

University of California, San Diego: The Department of Literature hosted a Graduate Student Enrichment event "MLA Mock Interview: A Dress Rehearsal." A panel of Literature faculty and graduate student recreated a complete MLA-style job interview, asking questions based on the "mock" candidates dissertation materials, followed by an open discussion and opportunity for graduate students to ask any questions about the job application and /or interview process.

University of Cincinnati: To enhance professional development opportunities for graduate students at UC, the Graduate School offered a pilot Graduate Teaching Fellowship Program to provide mentored teaching experiences for qualified students who might not normally have such an opportunity in their own discipline. To qualify, students had to be doctoral students who had successfully completed the "Becoming a More Effective Teacher" course offered in the Preparing Future Faculty program. Fellowship recipients were matched with outstanding teachers at the University for a mentored teaching experience over one academic quarter. This experience included actual teaching and lecturing with feedback, syllabus development, learning assessment, course content and materials selection, and, in general, active participation in course delivery. Fellows participated in bi-weekly meetings with other fellowship recipients and faculty facilitators. Each Teaching Fellow was awarded $3000. A total of 13 doctoral students participated in the pilot program… Overall the participants were very positive about their experience in this program. While all agreed that the program provided a good structure for a comprehensive teaching experience, and use of techniques learned in the PFF course, individual experiences varied based on the sustained commitment of both the student and the mentor. All participants strongly recommend continuing this program… [E]ncouraging results have led to in-progress collaboration with the Preparing Future Faculty Program where creative resources from both programs will be optimized to encourage students to complete their Ph.D.'s and attract them to the professoriate.

The pilot on enhanced teaching opportunities for graduate students was initiated with a special one-time allocation ($50K) to run this program… The challenge moving forward is to make the program attractive to both students and their advisors on its own merits; i.e., in the absence of a stipend supplement or with a reduced supplement. Additional challenges included attracting faculty to mentor students outside their programs, matching student and mentor interests and personalities, and maintaining a sustained level of participation from both the student and mentor through the pressures of an academic term.

CHAPTER 10
Next Steps for the Ph.D. Completion Project

This monograph has provided an overview of the interventions being implemented by the Phase II Research Partners to improve doctoral completion and reduce attrition. Based on a theoretical framework outlined in the 2004 CGS report that laid the foundation for the project, we categorized these interventions into six broad areas:

- Selection and admissions
- Mentoring and advising
- Financial support
- Research mode of the field
- Curricular and administrative processes and procedures
- Program environment

In each case, we provided an overview of the set of interventions being implemented and then illustrated specific examples drawn from the institutional proposals and annual progress reports.

While it is still too early to expect hard evidence linking the project activities to improved completion and reduced attrition rates in the doctoral programs participating in the project, anecdotal evidence from the institutions suggests that participation in the completion project has led to a number of cultural and programmatic changes in doctoral education.

First, there is a new realization of the need to develop and implement consistent definitions of key events in a doctoral program (such as entry, acceptance into candidacy, stop-out, drop-out, completion) and to design and deploy integrated data systems capable of housing linked data elements, tracking doctoral student progress over time, and being updated on a regular basis as new data become available. This has challenges, given that current data are housed in a variety of diverse systems that are often incompatible with one another.

Second, all of the institutions reported that participating in the Ph.D. Completion Project has led to the development of a "culture of evidence" wherein faculty and leaders across the institutions are paying attention to both the data coming out of the project as well as the need for evidence as a basis for making decisions, for improving the programs, and for improving the outcomes for their students. This new emphasis fits well within the current political and policy context of doctoral education which demands that institutions be accountable for their students.

Third, the institutions report that they are undertaking a variety of research efforts to better understand the factors affecting doctoral attrition and completion and to gather evidence about practices and programs that seem effective in stemming attrition. This has led to several innovative and much-needed interventions, as documented in the earlier chapters–ranging from early advising and peer mentoring to dissertation retreats. Hand-in-hand with this has come an increased sensitivity to issues facing students from underrepresented groups and the need to provide better mentoring and support networks for these students. None of this has been easy–institutions reported initial faculty resistance to change and a lack of willingness on part of both the students and faculty to participate in mentorship programs. Nonetheless, institutions are making considerable progress in these areas.

Fourth, the CGS project required participation across the SEM and SSH departments. As a result, the project has led to new conversations, discussions, and sharing of best practices among departments that normally tend to act as silos within an institution and an increased recognition that improving Ph.D. completion was an institution-wide endeavor.

As the project continues and additional data are collected and analyzed, CGS will study the impact of groups of interventions designed to improve completion rates. Some of these may prove to be most effective within specific fields and programs across most or all universities, whereas other interventions may work better in some institutional contexts than in others. While the project will probably be unable to isolate one strategy from all others as having a decisive effect on completion, there should be a demonstrable impact of groups of interventions on Ph.D. completion rates, and case studies will supplement the quantitative analysis.

The culminating publication in this series, scheduled for release in 2010, will include a comprehensive analysis of the quantitative and qualitative data submitted by the partnering universities in Phases I and II of the Ph.D. Completion Project, as well as a description of those policies and practices that appear to have had a demonstrated effect on completion rates and attrition patterns over time. We expect that the findings of the Ph.D. Completion Project will transform our understanding of the factors that contribute to higher Ph.D. completion rates nationwide, particularly for women and minorities.

APPENDIX A
Ph.D. Completion Project Advisory Board Members

CGS appointed an Advisory Board to guide the project. This group comprises individuals in leadership positions in academia, industry and research on graduate education.

Earl Lewis (Chair)
Executive VP for Academic Affairs & Provost
Emory University

John Benbow
Senior Principal Scientist
Pfizer Global R&D

James Duderstadt
President Emeritus/Professor of Science & Engineering
Director of the Millennium Project
University of Michigan

Gertrude Fraser
Vice Provost for Faculty Advancement
University of Virginia

Charlotte Kuh
Deputy Executive Director
The National Research Council

Joan Lorden
Provost
University of North Carolina-Charlotte

Michael Nettles
Senior Vice President
Policy, Evaluation & Research Center
ETS

Suzanne Ortega
Provost and Executive Vice President for Academic Affairs
University of New Mexico

Richard Shavelson
Professor of Education and Psychology
Stanford University

Barbara Williams
Senior Director, PGRD Staffing, Diversity and HR Planning
Pfizer Global R&D

APPENDIX B
Ph.D. Completion Project Institutions

Among the 46 proposals submitted by universities to participate in Phase I of the Ph.D. Completion Project (2004-2007), 21 universities were selected by an external advisory committee to receive grant funding as Research Partners based on the competitiveness of their proposals. The other 25 universities were included in the project as Project Partners. Many of these Project Partners voluntarily submitted data, and most of them actively participated in CGS sessions and events dedicated to the project and to issues of doctoral completion and attrition.

Phase I Research Partners:

Arizona State University
Cornell University
Duke University
Howard University
North Carolina State University
Princeton University
Purdue University
Université de Montréal (Canada)
University of California, Los Angeles
University of Cincinnati
University of Florida
University of Georgia
University of Illinois, Urbana–Champaign
University of Louisville
University of Maryland, Baltimore County
University of Michigan
University of Missouri–Columbia
University of North Carolina at Chapel Hill
University of Notre Dame
Washington University in St. Louis
Yale University

Phase I Project Partners:

Florida State University
Fordham University
George Washington University
Jackson State University
Louisiana State University
Marquette University
McGill University (Canada)
Michigan State University
New Mexico State University
New York University
North Dakota State University
Pennsylvania State University
Rutgers, the State University of New Jersey
Southern Illinois University Carbondale
Syracuse University
University of California, Berkeley
University of Colorado at Boulder
University of Iowa
University of Kansas
University of Melbourne (Australia)
University of Minnesota
University of Puerto Rico
University of Rhode Island
University of Southern California
Western Michigan University

In Phase II of the Ph.D. Completion Project (2007-2010), 22 universities were selected by an external advisory committee to receive grant funding as Research Partners based on the competitiveness of their proposals. Another 21 universities were included in the project as Project Partners. Many of these Project Partners voluntarily submitted data, and most of them actively participated in CGS sessions and events dedicated to the project and to issues of doctoral completion and attrition.

Phase II Research Partners:

Brown University
Cornell University
Duke University
Florida State University
Howard University
Marquette University
Michigan State University
North Carolina State University
Ohio State University
Pennsylvania State University
Purdue University
University of California, Los Angeles
University of California, San Diego
University of Cincinnati
University of Georgia
University of Illinois, Urbana-Champaign
University of Maryland, Baltimore County
University of Michigan
University of Missouri–Columbia
University of North Carolina at Chapel Hill
University of Southern California
Yale University

Phase II Project Partners:

Arizona State University
Colorado State University
Fordham University
Jackson State University
Loyola University Chicago
McMaster University (Canada)
Northwestern University
Princeton University
Rutgers, the State University of New Jersey
Syracuse University
University of Arkansas
University of California, Berkeley
University of Central Florida
University of Florida
University of Iowa
University of Kansas
University of Louisville
University of Melbourne (Australia)
University Notre Dame
University of Rhode Island
Washington University in St. Louis

REFERENCES

Bowen, W. G., & Rudenstine, N. L. (1992). *In pursuit of the PhD.* Princeton, NJ: Princeton University Press.

Council of Graduate Schools. (2004). *Ph.D. completion and attrition: Policy, numbers, leadership and next steps.* Washington, DC: Council of Graduate Schools.

Council of Graduate Schools. (2008a). *Ph.D. completion and attrition: Analysis of baseline program data from the Ph.D. Completion Project.* Washington, DC: Council of Graduate Schools.

Council of Graduate Schools. (2008b). *Ph.D. completion and attrition: Analysis of baseline demographic data from the Ph.D. Completion Project.* Washington, DC: Council of Graduate Schools.

Council of Graduate Schools. (2009). *Ph.D. completion and attrition: Findings from the Exit Surveys of Ph.D. Completers.* Washington, DC: Council of Graduate Schools.

de Valero, Y. F. (2001). "Departmental Factors Affecting Time-to-Degree and Completion Rates of doctoral Students at One Land-Grant Research Institution." *The Journal of Higher Education,* 72 (3), 341-367.

Lovitts, B. E. (2001). *Leaving the ivory tower: The causes and consequences of departure from doctoral study* (1st ed.). New York: Rowman and Littlefield Publishers, Inc.

Nelson, C., & Lovitts, B. E. (2001, June 29). 10 ways to keep graduate students from quitting. *The Chronicle of Higher Education,* p. B20.

Nerad, M., & Cerny, J. (1991). From facts to action: Expanding the graduate division's educational role. *CGS Communicator.* Special Edition (May).

Nettles, M. T., & Millett, C. M. (2006). *Three magic letters: Getting to Ph.D.* Baltimore: The Johns Hopkins University Press.

Walker, G; C. Golde; L. Jones, A.C. Bueschel, & P. Hutchings. (2008). *The Formation of Scholars: Rethinking Doctoral Education for the Twenty-First Century.* San Francisco: Jossey-Bass.